TO CRITICIZE THE CRITIC

By T. S. Eliot

verse

COLLECTED POEMS, 1909–1962

FOUR QUARTETS

THE CULTIVATION OF CHRISTMAS TREES

selected verse

SELECTED POEMS

THE WASTE LAND

children's verse

OLD POSSUM'S BOOK OF PRACTICAL CATS

plays

COLLECTED PLAYS

MURDER IN THE CATHEDRAL

THE FAMILY REUNION

THE COCKTAIL PARTY

THE CONFIDENTIAL CLERK

THE ELDER STATESMAN

literary criticism

SELECTED ESSAYS

THE USE OF POETRY AND THE USE OF CRITICISM

ON POETRY AND POETS

INTRODUCING JAMES JOYCE

ELIZABETHAN DRAMATISTS

TO CRITICIZE THE CRITIC

social criticism

THE IDEA OF A CHRISTIAN SOCIETY

NOTES TOWARDS THE DEFINITION OF CULTURE

philosophy

KNOWLEDGE AND EXPERIENCE in the philosophy of F. H. Bradley

T. S. Eliot

TO CRITICIZE THE CRITIC

and other writings

FARRAR, STRAUS & GIROUX • NEW YORK

First printing, 1965
Library of Congress catalog card number 65-25139
Printed in the United States of America

NOTE

Illness prevented my husband from revising 'To Criticize the Critic' and 'The Aims of Education' which are printed here exactly as he left them. Had he lived he would have incorporated further reflections into the former and written a similar review of his sociological writings. After delivering the Education lectures in Chicago he put them aside with the intention of expanding them into a book when the opportunity arose, but it never did.

In response to many requests he promised that 'Ezra Pound: His Metric and Poetry' and 'Reflections on *Vers Libre*' should be included in this collection.

V.E.

CONTENTS

TO CRITICIZE THE CRITIC

TO CRITICIZE THE CRITIC[1]

Of what use, or uses, is literary criticism, is a question worth asking again and again, even if we find no answer satisfactory. Criticism may be, what F. H. Bradley said of metaphysics, 'the finding of bad reasons for what we believe upon instinct, but to find these reasons is no less an instinct.' But as I propose to talk about my own criticism my choice of subject needs to be further defended. In casting an eye over my own literary criticism of the last forty-odd years, I hope that I may be able to draw some conclusions, some plausible generalizations of wider validity, or—what is still more worth while—stimulate other minds to do so; also I hope I may provoke other critics to make similar confessions. My justification must bet ha tthere is no other critic, living or dead, about whose work I am so well informed as I am about my own. I know more about the genesis of my essays and reviews than about those of any other critic; I know the chronology, the circumstances under which each essay was written and the motive for writing it, and about all those changes of attitude, taste, interest and belief which the years bring to pass. For the work of those masters of English criticism whom I regard with most reverence such full information is not available to me. I am thinking especially of Samuel Johnson and of Coleridge, and not ignoring Dryden or Arnold. But at this point I should distinguish between the several types of literary critic, in order to remind you that generalizations drawn from the study of the work of a critic of one type may not be applicable to that of others.

First of all among those types of critics other than mine, I should put down the Professional Critic—the writer whose literary criticism is his chief, perhaps his only title to fame. This critic

[1] The sixth Convocation Lecture delivered at the University of Leeds in July 1961.

might also be called the Super-Reviewer, for he has often been the official critic for some magazine or newspaper, and the occasion for each of his contributions the publication of some new book. The exemplar of this kind of criticism is of course the French critic Sainte-Beuve, who was the author of two important books, *Port-Royal* and *Chateaubriand et ses amis*, but the bulk of whose work consists of volume after volume of collected essays which had previously appeared week by week in the *feuilleton* of a newspaper. The Professional Critic may be, as Sainte-Beuve certainly was, a *failed* creative writer; and in the case of Sainte-Beuve it is certainly worth while to look at his poems, if one can come by them, as an aid to understanding why he wrote better about authors of the past than about his contemporaries. The Professional Critic however is not *necessarily* a failed poet, dramatist or novelist: so far as I know, my old friend in America, Paul Elmer More, whose Shelburne Essays have something of the monumental appearance of the *Causeries du lundi*, attempted no creative writing. Another old friend of mine who was a Professional Critic, of both books and theatre, Desmond MacCarthy, confined his literary activity to his weekly article or review and employed his leisure in delightful conversation instead of devoting it to the books he never wrote. And Edmund Gosse—a different case again: for it is not his industry as a critic, but one book of autobiography which is already a classic—*Father and Son*—that will perpetuate his name.

Second, I name the Critic with Gusto. This critic is not called to the seat of judgment; he is rather the advocate of the authors whose work he expounds, authors who are sometimes the forgotten or unduly despised. He calls our attention to such writers, helps us to see merit which we had overlooked and to find charm where we had expected only boredom. Of such was George Saintsbury, an erudite and genial man with an insatiable appetite for the second-rate, and a flair for discovering the excellence which is often to be found in the second-rate. Who but Saintsbury, in writing a book on the French Novel, would give far more pages to Paul de Kock than to Flaubert? There was also my old friend Charles Whibley: for example, read him on Sir

Thomas Urquhart or on Petronius. There was also Quiller-Couch, who must have taught many of those who attended his lectures at Cambridge, to find fresh sources of delight in English literature.

Third, the Academic and the Theoretical. I mention these two together, as they can overlap; but this category is perhaps too comprehensive, since it ranges from the purely scholarly, like W. P. Ker, who could illuminate an author of one age or language by an unexpected parallel with some author of another age or another language, to the philosophical critic, such as I. A. Richards and his disciple the philosophical critic William Empson. Mr. Richards and Mr. Empson are also poets, but I do not regard their work as a by-product of their poetry. And where are we to place other contemporaries, such as L. C. Knights or Wilson Knight, except as men who have combined teaching with original critical work? And another critic of importance, Dr. F. R. Leavis, who may be called the Critic as Moralist? The critic who is also tenant of an academic post is likely to have made a special study of one period or one author but to call him a Specialist Critic would seem a kind of abridgment of his right to examine whatever literature he pleases.

And finally we come to the critic whose criticism may be said to be a by-product of his creative activity. Particularly, the critic who is also a poet. Shall we say, the poet who has written some literary criticism? The condition of entrance into this category is that the candidate should be known primarily for his poetry, but that his criticism should be distinguished for its own sake, and not merely for any light it may throw upon its author's verse. And here I put Samuel Johnson, and Coleridge; and Dryden and Racine in their prefaces; and Matthew Arnold with reservations; and it is into this company that I must shyly intrude. I hope you need by now no further assurance that it was not laziness that impelled me to turn to my own writings for my material. It most certainly was not vanity: for when I first applied myself to the required reading for this address, it was so long since I had read many of my essays that I approached them with apprehension rather than with hopeful expectations.

I am happy to say that I did not find quite so much to be ashamed of as I had feared. There are, to be sure, statements with which I no longer agree; there are views which I maintain with less firmness of conviction than when I first expressed them, or which I maintain only with important reservations; there are statements the meaning of which I no longer understand. There may be areas in which my knowledge has increased; there are areas in which my knowledge has evaporated. On re-reading my essay on Pascal, for instance, I was astonished at the extent of the information I seem to have possessed when I wrote it. And there are some matters in which I have simply lost interest, so that, if asked whether I still hold the same belief, I could only say 'I don't know' or 'I don't care'. There are errors of judgment, and, what I regret more, there are errors of tone: the occasional note of arrogance, of vehemence, of cocksureness or rudeness, the braggadocio of the mild-mannered man safely entrenched behind his typewriter. Yet I must acknowledge my relationship to the man who made those statements, and in spite of all these exceptions, I continue to identify myself with the author.

Even in saying that, however, I think of a qualification. I find myself constantly irritated by having my words, perhaps written thirty or forty years ago, quoted as if I had uttered them yesterday. One very intelligent expositor of my work, who regarded it, furthermore, with a very favourable eye, discussed my critical writings some years ago as if I had, at the outset of my career as a literary critic, sketched out the design for a massive critical structure, and spent the rest of my life filling in the details. When I publish a collection of essays, or whenever I allow an essay to be re-published elsewhere, I make a point of indicating the original date of publication, as a reminder to the reader of the distance of time that separates the author when he wrote it from the author as he is today. But rare is the writer who, quoting me, says 'this is what Mr. Eliot thought (or felt) in 1933' (or whatever the date was). Every writer is accustomed to seeing his words quoted out of context, in such a way as to put an unintended construction upon them, by not over-scrupulous controversialists. But the quotation of pronouncements of many years ago, as if they had been made yesterday, is still more frequent, because it is most often wholly without malice. I will give one instance of a statement which has continued to dog its author long after it has ceased, in his opinion, to be a satisfactory statement of his beliefs. It is a sentence from the preface to a small collection of essays entitled *For Lancelot Andrewes*, to the effect that I was a classicist in literature, a royalist in politics, and an Anglo-Catholic in religion. I ought to have foreseen that so quotable a sentence would follow me through life as Shelley tells us his thoughts followed him:

> And his own thoughts, along that rugged way,
> Pursued, like raging hounds, their father and their prey.

The sentence in question was provoked by a personal experience. My old teacher and master, Irving Babbitt, to whom I owe so much, stopped in London on his way back to Harvard from Paris, where he had been lecturing, and he and Mrs. Babbitt dined with me. I had not seen Babbitt for some years, and I felt obliged to acquaint him with a fact as yet unknown to my small circle of readers (for this was I think in the year 1927) that I had recently been baptized and confirmed into the Church of England. I knew that it would come as a shock to him to learn that any disciple of his had so turned his coat, though he had already had what must have been a much greater shock when his close friend and ally Paul Elmer More defected from Humanism to Christianity. But all Babbitt said was: 'I think you should come out into the open.' I may have been a little nettled by this remark; the quotable sentence turned up in the preface to the book of essays I had in preparation, swung into orbit, and has been circling my little world ever since. Well, my religious beliefs are unchanged, and I am strongly in favour of the maintenance of the monarchy in all countries which have a monarchy; as for Classicism and Romanticism, I find that the terms have no longer the importance to me that they once had. But even if my statement of belief needed no qualification at all after the passage of the years, I should not be inclined to express it in quite this way.

So far as I can judge, from references, quotations and reprints in anthologies, it is my earlier essays which have made the deeper impression. I attribute this to two causes. The first is the dogmatism of youth. When we are young we see issues sharply defined: as we age we tend to make more reservations, to qualify our positive assertions, to introduce more parentheses. We see objections to our own views, we regard the enemy with greater tolerance and even sometimes with sympathy. When we are young, we are confident in our opinions, sure that we possess the whole truth; we are enthusiastic, or indignant. And readers, even mature readers, are attracted to a writer who is quite sure of himself. The second reason for the enduring popularity of some of my early criticism is less easily apprehended, especially by readers of a younger generation. It is that in my earlier criticism, both in my general affirmations about poetry and in writing about authors who had influenced me, I was implicitly defending the sort of poetry that I and my friends wrote. This gave my essays a kind of urgency, the warmth of appeal of the advocate, which my later, more detached and I hope more judicial essays cannot claim. I was in reaction, not only against Georgian poetry, but against Georgian criticism; I was writing in a context which the reader of today has either forgotten, or has never experienced.

In a lecture on Johnson's *Lives of the Poets*, published in one of my collections of essays and addresses,[1] I made the point that in appraising the judgments of any critic of a past age, one needed to see him in the context of that age, to try to place oneself at his point of view. This is a difficult effort for the imagination; one, indeed, in which we cannot hope for more than partial success. We cannot discount the influence upon our formation of the creative writing and the critical writing of the intervening generations, or the inevitable modifications of taste, or our greater knowledge and understanding of the literature preceding that of the age which we are trying to understand. Yet merely to make that effort of imagination, and to have these difficulties in mind, is worth our while. In reviewing my own early criticism, I am struck by the degree to which it was conditioned by the state of literature at the time at which it was written, as well as by the stage of maturity at which I had arrived, by the influences to which I

[1] *On Poetry and Poets* (Faber & Faber, 1957).

had been exposed, and by the occasion of each essay. I cannot myself bring to mind all these circumstances, reconstruct all the conditions under which I wrote: how much less can any future critic of my work have knowledge of them, or, if he has knowledge have understanding, or if he has both knowledge and understanding, find my essays of the same interest that they had for those who read them sympathetically when they first appeared? No literary criticism can for a future generation excite more than curiosity, unless it continues to be of use in itself to future generations, to have intrinsic value out of its historical context. But if any part of it does have this timeless value, then we shall appreciate that value all the more precisely if we also attempt to put ourselves at the point of view of the writer and his first readers. To study the criticism of Johnson or of Coleridge in this way is undoubtedly rewarding.

I can divide my own critical writing roughly into three periods. There was first the period of *The Egoist*, that remarkable bi-weekly edited and published by Miss Harriet Weaver. Richard Aldington had been sub-editor, and when he was called up for military service in the First World War Ezra Pound nominated me to Miss Weaver to fill his place. In *The Egoist* appeared an essay called *Tradition and the Individual Talent*, which still enjoys immense popularity among those editors who prepare anthological text-books for American college students. There were then two influences which are not so incongruous as might at first sight appear: that of Irving Babbitt and that of Ezra Pound. The influence of Pound at that time may be detected in references to Remy de Gourmont, in my papers on Henry James, an author whom Pound much admired, but for whom my own enthusiasm has somewhat flagged, and sundry allusions to authors, such as Gavin Douglas, whose work I hardly knew. The influence of Babbitt (with an infusion later of T. E. Hulme and of the more literary essays of Charles Maurras) is apparent in my recurrent theme of Classicism versus Romanticism. In my second period, after 1918, when *The Egoist* had come to an end, I was writing essays and reviews for two editors in whom I was fortunate, for they both gave me always the right books to review: Middleton Murry in the short-lived *Athenaeum*, and Bruce Richmond in *The Times Literary Supplement*. Most of my contributions remain buried in the files of these two papers, but the best, and they are among the best of my essays, are reprinted in my collections. My third period has been, for one reason or another, one of public lectures and addresses rather than of articles and reviews.

And here I wish to draw what seems to me an important line of demarcation between the essays of generalization (such as *Tradition and the Individual Talent*) and appreciations of individual authors. It is those in the latter category which seem to me to have the best chance of retaining some value for future readers: and I wonder whether this assertion does not itself imply a generalization applicable to other critics of my type. But I must draw a distinction here too. Several years ago my New York publishers brought out a paper-back selection of my essays on Elizabethan and Jacobean drama. I made the selection myself, and wrote a preface explaining my choice. I found that the essays with which I was still pleased were those on the contemporaries of Shakespeare, not those on Shakespeare himself. It was from these minor dramatists that I, in my own poetic formation, had learned my lessons; it was by them, and not by Shakespeare, that my imagination had been stimulated, my sense of rhythm trained, and my emotions fed. I had read them at the age at which they were best suited to my temperament and stage of development, and had read them with passionate delight long before I had any thought, or any opportunity of writing about them. At the period in which the stirrings of desire to write verse were becoming insistent, these were the men whom I took as my tutors. Just as the modern poet who influenced me was not Baudelaire but Jules Laforgue, so the dramatic poets were Marlowe and Webster and Tourneur and Middleton and Ford, not Shakespeare. A poet of the supreme greatness of Shakespeare can hardly influence, he can only be imitated: and the difference between influence and imitation is that influence can fecundate, whereas imitation—especially unconscious imitation—can only sterilize. (But when I came to attempt one brief imitation of Dante I was fifty-five years old and knew exactly what I was doing.) Besides, imitation of a writer in a foreign language can often be profitable—because we cannot succeed.

So much for those of my essays in literary criticism which I think have the best chance of survival, in the sense that they are those which have, I believe, the best chance of giving pleasure, and possibly enlarging the understanding, on the part of future readers, of the authors criticized. Now what of the generalizations, and the phrases which have flourished, such as 'dissociation of sensibility' and 'objective correlative'? I think also of an article on 'the function of criticism' written for *The Criterion*. I am not sure, at this distance of time, how valid are the two phrases I have just cited: I am always at a loss what to say, when earnest scholars, or schoolchildren, write to ask me for an explanation. The term 'objective correlative' occurs in an essay on *Hamlet and his Problems* in which I was perhaps not altogether guiltless of trailing my coat: I was at that time hand-in-glove with that gallant controversialist, J. M. Robertson, in his critical studies of Tudor and Stuart drama. But whatever the future of these phrases, and even if I am unable to defend them now with any forensic plausibility, I think they have been useful in their time. They have been accepted, they have been rejected, they may soon go out of fashion completely: but they have served their turn as stimuli to the critical thinking of others. And literary criticism, as I hinted at the beginning, is an instinctive activity of the civilized mind. But I prophesy that if my phrases are given consideration, a century hence, it will be only in their historical context, by scholars interested in the mind of my generation.

What I wish to suggest, however, is that these phrases may be accounted for as being conceptual symbols for emotional preferences. Thus, the emphasis on tradition came about, I believe, as a result of my reaction against the poetry, in the English language, of the nineteenth and early twentieth centuries, and my passion for the poetry, both dramatic and lyric, of the late sixteenth and early seventeenth centuries. The 'objective correlative' in the essay on Hamlet may stand for my bias towards the more mature plays of Shakespeare—*Timon*, *Antony and Cleopatra*, *Coriolanus* notably—and towards those late plays of Shakespeare about which Mr.

Wilson Knight has written illuminatingly. And the 'dissociation of sensibility' may represent my devotion to Donne and the metaphysical poets, and my reaction against Milton.

It seems to me, in fact, that these concepts, these generalizations, had their origin in my sensibility. They arise from my feeling of kinship with one poet or with one kind of poetry rather than another. I ought not to claim that what I am now saying holds good of other types of critic than mine, or even of other critics of the type to which I myself belong—that is, of poets who have also written critical essays. But about any writer in the field of aesthetics I always incline to ask: 'what literary works, paintings, sculpture, architecture and music does this theorist really enjoy?' We can, of course—and this is a danger to which the philosophical critic of art may be exposed—adopt a theory and then persuade ourselves that we like the works of art that fit into that theory. But I am sure that my own theorizing has been epiphenomenal of my tastes, and that in so far as it is valid, it springs from direct experience of those authors who have profoundly influenced my own writing. I am aware, of course, that my 'objective correlative' and my 'dissociation of sensibility' must be attacked or defended on their own level of abstraction, and that I have done no more than indicate what I believe to have been their genesis. I am also aware that in accounting for them in this way I am now making a generalization about my generalizations. But I am certain of one thing: that I have written best about writers who have influenced my own poetry. And I say 'writers' and not only 'poets', because I include F. H. Bradley, whose works—I might say whose personality as manifested in his works—affected me profoundly; and Bishop Lancelot Andrewes, from one of whose sermons on the Nativity I lifted several lines of my *Journey of the Magi* and of whose prose there may be a faint reflection in the sermon in *Murder in the Cathedral*. I include, in fact, any writers whether of verse or prose, whose style has strongly affected my own. I have hope that such essays of mine on individual writers who have influenced me, may retain some value even for a future generation which will reject or ridicule my theories. I spent three years, when young, in the study of philosophy. What remains to me of these studies? The style of three philosophers: Bradley's English, Spinoza's Latin and Plato's Greek.

It is in relation to essays on individual poets that I come to consider the question: how far can the critic alter public taste for one or another poet or one or another period of literature of the past? Have I myself, for example, been to any degree responsible for arousing interest and promoting appreciation of the early dramatists or of the metaphysical poets? I should say, hardly at all—as critic. We must distinguish of course between *taste* and *fashion*. Fashion, the love of change for its own sake, the desire for something new, is very transient; *taste* is something that springs from a deeper source. In a language in which great poetry has been written for many generations, as it has in ours, each generation will vary in its preferences among the classics of that language. Some writers of the past will respond to the taste of the living generations more nearly than others; some periods of the past may have closer affinity to our own age than others. To a young reader, or a critic of crude taste, the authors whom his generation favours may seem to be better than those fancied by the previous generation; the more conscious critic may recognize that they are simply more congenial, but not necessarily of greater merit. It is one function of the critic to assist the literate public of his day to recognize its affinity with one poet, or with one type of poetry, or one age of poetry, rather than with another.

The critic, however, cannot create a taste. I have sometimes been credited with starting the vogue for Donne and other metaphysical poets, as well as for the minor Elizabethan and Jacobean dramatists. But I did not discover any of these poets. Coleridge, and Browning in turn, admired Donne; and as for the early dramatists, there is Lamb, and the enthusiastic tributes of Swinburne are by no means without critical merit. In our own time, John Donne has lacked no publicity: Gosse's *Life and Letters*, in two volumes, appeared in 1899. I remember being introduced to Donne's poetry when I was a Freshman at Harvard by Professor Briggs, an ardent admirer; Grierson's edition of the Poems, in two volumes, was published in 1912; and it was Grierson's *Metaphysical Poetry*, sent me to review, that gave me my first occasion to write about Donne. I think that if I wrote well about the metaphysical poets, it was because they were poets who had inspired me. And if I can be said to have had any influence whatever in promoting a wider interest in them, it was simply because no previous poet who had praised these poets had been so deeply influenced by them as I had been. As the taste for my own poetry spread, so did the taste for the poets to whom I owed the greatest debt and about whom I had written. Their poetry, and mine, were congenial to that age. I sometimes wonder whether that age is not coming to an end.

It is true that I owed, and have always acknowledged, an equally great debt to certain French poets of the late nineteenth century, about whom I have never written. I have written about Baudelaire, but nothing about Jules Laforgue, to whom I owe more than to any one poet in any language, or about Tristan Corbière, to whom I owe something also. The reason, I believe, is that no one commissioned me to do so. For these early essays were all written for money, which I needed, and the occasion was always a new book about an author, a new edition of his works, or an anniversary.

The question of the extent to which a critic may influence the taste of his time I have answered, speaking for myself alone, by saying that I do not believe that my own criticism has had, or could have had, any influence whatever apart from my own poems. Let me turn now to the question: how far, and in what ways do the critic's own tastes and views alter in the course of his lifetime? To what extent do such changes indicate greater maturity, when do they indicate decay, and when must we consider them merely as changes–neither for better nor for worse? For myself, again, I find that my opinion of poets whose work influenced me in my formative stage remains unchanged, and I abate nothing of the praise I have given them. True, they do not now give me that intense excitement and sense of enlargement and liberation which comes from a discovery which is also a discovery of oneself: but that is an experience which can only happen once. And indeed it is to other poets than these that I am likely to turn now for pure delight. I turn more often the pages of Mallarmé than those of Laforgue, those of George Herbert than those of Donne, of Shakespeare than of his contemporaries and epigoni. This does not necessarily involve a judgment of relative greatness: it is merely that what has best responded to my need in middle and later age is different from the nourishment I needed in my youth. So great is Shakespeare, however, that a lifetime is hardly enough for growing up to appreciate him. There is one poet, however, who impressed me profoundly when I was twenty-two and with only a rudimentary acquaintance with his language started to puzzle out his lines, one poet who remains the comfort and amazement of my age, although my knowledge of his language remains rudimentary. I was never more than an inferior classical scholar: the poet I speak of is Dante. In my youth, I think that Dante's astonishing economy and directness of language—his arrow that goes unerringly to the centre of the target—provided for me a wholesome corrective to the extravagances of the Elizabethan, Jacobean and Caroline authors in whom I also delighted.

Perhaps what I want to say now is true of all literary criticism. I am sure that it is true of mine, that it is at its best when I have been writing of authors whom I have wholeheartedly admired. And my next best are of authors whom I greatly admire, but only with qualifications with which other critics may disagree. I do not ask to be reassured about my essays on minor Elizabethan dramatists, but am always interested to hear what other critics of poetry think, for instance, about what I have written on Tennyson or Byron. As for criticism of negligible authors, it can hardly be of permanent interest, because people will cease to be interested in the writers criticized. And censure of a great writer—or a writer whose works have had the test of time—is likely to be influenced by other than literary considerations. The personality of Milton, as well as some of his politics and theology, was obviously antipathetic to Samuel Johnson, as it is to me. (But when I wrote my first essay on Milton, I was considering his poetry as poetry and in relation to what I conceived to be the needs of my own time; and when I wrote my second essay on Milton I did not intend it to be, what Desmond MacCarthy and others took it to be, a recantation of my earlier opinion, but a development in view of the fact that there was no longer any likelihood of his being imitated, and that therefore he could profitably be studied. This reference to Milton is parenthetical.) I do not regret what I have written about Milton: but when an author's mind is so antipathetic to my own as was that of Thomas Hardy, I wonder whether it might not have been better never to have written about him at all.

Perhaps my judgment is less assured about writers who are contemporary or nearly so, than about writers of the past. Yet my valuation of the work of those poets contemporary with me, and of those poets younger than myself with whom I feel an affinity, remains unchanged. There is however one contemporary figure about whom my mind will, I fear, always waver between dislike, exasperation, boredom and admiration. That is D. H. Lawrence.

My opinions of D. H. Lawrence seem to form a tissue of praise and execration. The more vehement of my ejaculations of dislike are preserved, like flies in amber, or like wasps in honey, by the diligence of Dr. Leavis; but between two passages which he quotes, one published in 1927 and the other in 1933, I find that in 1931 I was wagging my finger rather pompously at the bishops who had assembled at the Lambeth Conference, and reproaching them for 'missing an opportunity for dissociating themselves from the condemnation of two very serious and improving writers'—namely, Mr. James Joyce and Mr. D. H. Lawrence. I cannot account for such apparent contradictions. Last year, in the *Lady Chatterley* case, I expressed my readiness to appear as a witness for the defence. Perhaps the counsel for the defence were well advised not to put me into the witness box, as it might have been rather difficult to make my views clear to a jury by that form of inquisition, and a really wily prosecutor might have tied me up in knots. I felt then, as I feel now, that the prosecution of such a book—a book of most serious and highly moral *intention*—was a deplorable blunder, the consequences of which would be most unfortunate whatever the verdict, and give the book a kind of vogue which would have been abhorrent to the author. But my antipathy to the author remains, on the ground of what seems to me egotism, a strain of cruelty, and a failing in common with Thomas Hardy—the lack of a sense of humour.

My particular reason for referring to my response to the work of Lawrence is that it is well to remind ourselves, in discussing the subject of literary criticism, that we cannot escape personal bias, and that there are other standards besides that of 'literary merit', which cannot be excluded. It was noticeable, in the Chatterley case, that some witnesses for the defence defended the book for the moral intentions of the author rather than on the ground of its being important as a work of literature.

In most of what I have been saying today, however, I have endeavoured to confine myself to that part of my own critical prose which is most nearly definable as '*literary* criticism'. May I sum up the conclusions to which I have come, after re-reading all of my writing which can be covered by that designation? I have found that my best work falls within rather narrow limits, my best essays being, in my opinion, those concerned with writers who had influenced me in my poetry; naturally the majority of these writers were poets. And it is that part of my criticism concerned with writers towards whom I felt gratitude and whom I could praise wholeheartedly, which is the part in which I continue to feel most confidence as the years pass. And as for the phrases of generalization which have been so often quoted, I am convinced that their force comes from the fact that they are attempts to summarize, in conceptual form, direct and intense experience of the poetry that I have found most congenial.

It is risky, and perhaps presumptuous, for me to generalize from my own experience, even about critics of my own type—that is, writers who are primarily creative but reflect upon their own vocation and upon the work of other practitioners. I am, I admit, much more interested in what other poets have written about poetry than in what critics who are not poets have said about it. I have suggested also that it is impossible to fence off *literary* criticism from criticism on other grounds, and that moral, religious and social judgments cannot be wholly excluded. That they can, and that literary merit can be estimated in complete isolation, is the illusion of those who believe that literary merit alone can justify the publication of a book which could otherwise be condemned on moral grounds. But the nearest we get to pure literary criticism is the criticism of artists writing about their own art; and for this I turn to Johnson, and Wordsworth and Coleridge. (Paul Valéry's is a special case.) In other types of criticism, the historian, the philosopher, the moralist, the sociologist, the grammarian may play a large part; but in so far as literary criticism is purely literary, I believe that the criticism of artists writing about their own art is of greater intensity, and carries more authority, though the area of the artist's competence may be much narrower. I feel that I myself have spoken with authority (if the phrase itself does not suggest arrogance) only about those authors—poets and a very few prose writers—who have influenced me; that on poets who have not influenced me I still deserve serious consideration; and that on authors whose work I dislike my views may—to say the least—be highly disputable. And I should remind you again, in closing, that I have directed attention on my literary criticism *qua* literary, and that a study in respect of my religious, social, political or moral beliefs, and of that large part of my prose writing which is directly concerned with these beliefs would be quite another exercise in self-examination. But I hope that what I have said today may suggest reasons why, as the critic grows older, his critical writings may be less fired by enthusiasm, but informed by wider interest and, one hopes, by greater wisdom and humility.

FROM POE TO VALÉRY[1]

What I attempt here is not a judicial estimate of Edgar Allan Poe; I am not trying to decide his rank as a poet or to isolate his essential originality. Poe is indeed a stumbling block for the judicial critic. If we examine his work in detail, we seem to find in it nothing but slipshod writing, puerile thinking unsupported by wide reading or profound scholarship, haphazard experiments in various types of writing, chiefly under pressure of financial need, without perfection in any detail. This would not be just. But if, instead of regarding his work analytically, we take a distant view of it as a whole, we see a mass of unique shape and impressive size to which the eye constantly returns. Poe's influence is equally puzzling. In France the influence of his poetry and of his poetic theories has been immense. In England and America it seems almost negligible. Can we point to any poet whose style appears to have been formed by a study of Poe? The only one whose name immediately suggests itself is—Edward Lear. And yet one cannot be sure that one's own writing has *not* been influenced by Poe. I can name positively certain poets whose work has influenced me, I can name others whose work, I am sure, has not; there may be still others of whose influence I am unaware, but whose influence I might be brought to acknowledge; but about Poe I shall never be sure. He wrote very few poems, and of those few only half a dozen have had a great success: but those few are as well known to as large a number of people, are as well remembered by everybody, as any poems ever written. And some of his tales have had an important influence upon authors, and in types of writing where such influence would hardly be expected.

[1] A lecture delivered at the Library of Congress, Washington, on Friday November 19th, 1948.

I shall here make no attempt to explain the enigma. At most, this is a contribution to the study of his influence; and an elucidation, partial as it may be, of one cause of Poe's importance in the light of that influence. I am trying to look at him, for a moment, as nearly as I can, through the eyes of three French poets, Baudelaire, Mallarmé and especially Paul Valéry. The sequence is itself important. These three French poets represent the beginning, the middle and the end of a particular tradition in poetry. Mallarmé once told a friend of mine that he came to Paris because he wanted to know Baudelaire; that he had once seen him at a bookstall on a quai, but had not had the courage to accost him. As for Valéry, we know from the first letter to Mallarmé, written when he was hardly more than a boy, of his discipleship of the elder poet; and we know of his devotion to Mallarmé until Mallarmé's death. Here are three literary generations, representing almost exactly a century of French poetry. Of course, these are poets very different from each other; of course, the literary progeny of Baudelaire was numerous and important, and there are other lines of descent from him. But I think we can trace the development and descent of one particular theory of the nature of poetry through these three poets and it is a theory which takes its origin in the theory, still more than in the practice, of Edgar Poe. And the impression we get of the influence of Poe is the more impressive, because of the fact that Mallarmé, and Valéry in turn, did not merely derive from Poe through Baudelaire: each of them subjected himself to that influence directly, and has left convincing evidence of the value which he attached to the theory and practice of Poe himself. Now, we all of us like to believe that we understand our own poets better than any foreigner can do; but I think we should be prepared to entertain the possibility that these Frenchmen have seen something in Poe that English-speaking readers have missed.

My subject, then, is not simply Poe but Poe's effect upon three French poets, representing three successive generations; and my purpose is also to approach an understanding of a peculiar attitude towards poetry, by the poets themselves, which is perhaps the most interesting, possibly the most characteristic, and certainly the most original development of the aesthetic of verse made in that period as a whole. It is all the more worthy of examination if, as I incline to believe, this attitude towards poetry represents a phase which has come to an end with the death of Valéry. For our study of it should help towards the understanding of whatever it may be that our generation and the next will find to take its place.

Before concerning myself with Poe as he appeared in the eyes of these French poets, I think it as well to present my own impression of his status among American and English readers and critics; for, if I am wrong, you may have to criticize what I say of his influence in France with my errors in mind. It does not seem to me unfair to say that Poe has been regarded as a minor, or secondary, follower of the Romantic Movement: a successor to the so-called 'Gothic' novelists in his fiction, and a follower of Byron and Shelley in his verse. This however is to place him in the English tradition; and there certainly he does not belong. English readers sometimes account for that in Poe which is outside of any English tradition, by saying that it is American; but this does not seem to me wholly true either, especially when we consider the other American writers of his own and an earlier generation. There is a certain flavour of provinciality about his work, in a sense in which Whitman is not in the least provincial: it is the provinciality of the person who is not at home where he belongs, but cannot get to anywhere else. Poe is a kind of displaced European; he is attracted to Paris, to Italy and to Spain, to places which he could endow with romantic gloom and grandeur. Although his ambit of movement hardly extended beyond the limits of Richmond and Boston longitudinally, and neither east nor west of these centres, he seems a wanderer with no fixed abode. There can be few authors of such eminence who have drawn so little from their own roots, who have been so isolated from any surroundings.

I believe the view of Poe taken by the ordinary cultivated English or American reader is something like this: Poe is the author of a few, a very few short poems which enchanted him for a time when he was a boy, and which do somehow stick in the memory. I do not think that he re-reads these poems, unless he turns to them in the pages of an anthology; his enjoyment of them is rather the memory of an enjoyment which he may for a moment recapture. They seem to him to belong to a particular period when his interest in poetry had just awakened. Certain images, and still more certain rhythms, abide with him. This reader also remembers certain of the tales–not very many–and holds the opinion that *The Gold Bug* was quite good for its times, but that detective fiction has made great strides since then. And he may sometimes contrast him with Whitman, having frequently re-read Whitman, but not Poe.

As for the prose, it is recognized that Poe's tales had great influence upon some types of popular fiction. So far as detective fiction is concerned, nearly everything can be traced to two authors: Poe and Wilkie Collins. The two influences sometimes concur, but are also responsible for two different types of detective. The efficient professional policeman originates with Collins, the brilliant and eccentric amateur with Poe. Conan Doyle owes much to Poe, and not merely to Monsieur Dupin of *The Murders in the Rue Morgue*. Sherlock Holmes was deceiving Watson when he told him that he had bought his Stradivarius violin for a few shillings at a second-hand shop in the Tottenham Court Road. He found that violin in the ruins of the house of Usher. There is a close similarity between the musical exercises of Holmes and those of Roderick Usher: those wild and irregular improvisations which, although on one occasion they sent Watson off to sleep, must have been excruciating to any ear trained to music. It seems to me probable that the romances of improbable and incredible adventure of Rider Haggard found their inspiration in Poe–and Haggard himself had imitators enough. I think it equally likely that H. G. Wells, in his early romances of scientific exploration and invention, owed much to the stimulus of some of Poe's narratives–*Gordon Pym*, or *A Descent into the Maelstrom* for example, or *The Facts in the Case of Monsieur Valdemar*. The compilation of evidence I leave to those who are interested to pursue the inquiry. But I fear that nowadays too few readers open *She* or *The War of the Worlds* or *The Time Machine*: fewer still are capable of being thrilled by their predecessors.

What strikes me first, as a general difference between the way in which the French poets whom I have cited took Poe, and the way of American and English critics of equivalent authority, is the attitude of the former towards Poe's *œuvre*, towards his work as a whole. Anglo-Saxon critics are, I think, more inclined to make separate judgments of the different parts of an author's work. We regard Poe as a man who dabbled in verse and in kinds of prose, without settling down to make a thoroughly good job of any one *genre*. These French readers were impressed by the variety of form of expression, because they found, or thought they found, an essential unity; while admitting, if necessary, that much of the work is fragmentary or occasional, owing to circumstances of poverty, frailty and vicissitude, they nevertheless take him as an author of such seriousness that his work must be grasped as a whole. This represents partly a difference between two kinds of critical mind; but we must claim, for our own view, that it is supported by our awareness of the blemishes and imperfections of Poe's actual writing. It is worth while to illustrate these faults, as they strike an English-speaking reader.

Poe had, to an exceptional degree, the feeling for the incantatory element in poetry, of that which may, in the most nearly literal sense, be called 'the magic of verse'. His versification is not, like that of the greatest masters of prosody, of the kind which yields a richer melody, through study and long habituation, to the maturing sensibility of the reader returning to it at times throughout his life. Its effect is immediate and undeveloping; it is probably much the same for the sensitive schoolboy and for the ripe mind and cultivated ear. In this unchanging immediacy, it partakes perhaps more of the character of very good *verse* than of poetry—but that is to start a hare which I have no intention of following here, for it is, I am sure, 'poetry' and not 'verse'. It has the effect of an incantation which, because of its very crudity, stirs the feelings at a deep and almost primitive level. But, in his choice of the word which has the right *sound*, Poe is by no means careful that it should have also the right *sense*. I will give one comparison of uses of the same word by Poe and by Tennyson—who, of all English poets since Milton, had probably the most accurate and fastidious appreciation of the sound of syllables. In Poe's *Ulalume*—to my mind one of his most successful, as well as typical, poems—we find the lines

It was night, in the lonesome October
Of my most immemorial year.

Immemorial, according to the Oxford Dictionary, means: 'that is beyond memory or out of mind; ancient beyond memory or record: extremely old.' None of these meanings seems applicable to this use of the word by Poe. The year was not beyond memory—the speaker remembers one incident in it very well; at the conclusion he even remembers a funeral in the same place just a year earlier. The line of Tennyson, equally well known, and justly admired because the sound of the line responds so well to the sound which the poet wishes to evoke, may already have come to mind:

The moan of doves in immemorial elms.

Here *immemorial*, besides having the most felicitous sound value, is exactly the word for trees so old that no one knows just how old they are.

Poetry, of different kinds, may be said to range from that in which the attention of the reader is directed primarily to the sound, to that in which it is directed primarily to the sense. With the former kind, the sense may be apprehended almost unconsciously; with the latter kind—at these two extremes—it is the sound, of the operation of which upon us we are unconscious. But, with either type, sound and sense must cooperate; in even the most purely incantatory poem, the dictionary meaning of words cannot be disregarded with impunity.

An irresponsibility towards the meaning of words is not infrequent with Poe. *The Raven* is, I think, far from being Poe's best poem; though, partly because of the analysis which the author gives in *The Philosophy of Composition*, it is the best known.

In there stepped a stately Raven of the saintly days of yore,

Since there is nothing particularly saintly about the raven, if indeed the ominous bird is not wholly the reverse, there can be no point in referring his origin to a period of saintliness, even if such a period can be assumed to have existed. We have just heard the raven described as *stately*; but we are told presently that he is *ungainly*, an attribute hardly to be reconciled, without a good deal of explanation, with *stateliness*. Several words in the poem seem to be inserted either merely to fill out the line to the required measure, or for the sake of a rhyme. The bird is addressed as 'no craven' quite needlessly, except for the pressing need of a rhyme to 'raven'–a surrender to the exigencies of rhyme with which I am sure Malherbe would have had no patience. And there is not always even such schoolboy justification as this: to say that the lamplight 'gloated o'er' the sofa cushions is a freak of fancy which, even were it relevant to have a little gloating going on somewhere, would appear forced.

Imperfections in *The Raven* such as these–and one could give others–may serve to explain why *The Philosophy of Composition*, the essay in which Poe professes to reveal his method in composing *The Raven*–has not been taken so seriously in England or America as in France. It is difficult for us to read that essay without reflecting, that if Poe plotted out his poem with such calculation, he might have taken a little more pains over it: the result hardly does credit to the method. Therefore we are likely to draw the conclusion that Poe in analysing his poem was practising either a hoax, or a piece of self-deception in setting down the way in which he wanted to think that he had written it. Hence the essay has not been taken so seriously as it deserves.

Poe's other essays in poetic aesthetic deserve consideration also. No poet, when he writes his own *art poétique*, should hope to do much more than explain, rationalize, defend or prepare the way for his own practice: that is, for writing his own kind of poetry. He may think that he is establishing laws for all poetry; but what he has to say that is worth saying has its immediate relation to the way in which he himself writes or wants to write: though it may well be equally valid to his immediate juniors, and extremely helpful to them. We are only safe in finding, in his writing about poetry, principles valid for any poetry, so long as we check what he says by the kind of poetry he writes. Poe has a remarkable passage about the impossibility of writing a long poem—for a long poem, he holds, is at best a series of short poems strung together. What we have to bear in mind is that he himself was incapable of writing a long poem. He could conceive only a poem which was a single simple effect: for him, the whole of a poem had to be in one mood. Yet it is only in a poem of some length that a variety of moods can be expressed; for a variety of moods requires a number of different themes or subjects, related either in themselves or in the mind of the poet. These parts can form a whole which is more than the sum of the parts; a whole such that the pleasure we derive from the reading of any part is enhanced by our grasp of the whole. It follows also that in a long poem some parts may be deliberately planned to be less 'poetic' than others: these passages may show no lustre when extracted, but may be intended to elicit, by contrast, the significance of other parts, and to unite them into a whole more significant than any of the parts. A long poem may gain by the widest possible variations of intensity. But Poe wanted a poem to be of the first intensity throughout: it is questionable whether he could have appreciated the more philosophical passages in Dante's *Purgatorio*. What Poe had said has proved in the past of great comfort to other poets equally incapable of the long poem; and we must recognize that the question of the possibility of writing a long poem is not simply that of the strength and staying power of the individual poet, but may have to do with the conditions of the age in which he find himself. And what Poe has to say on the subject is illuminating, in helping us to understand the point of view of poets for whom the long poem is impossible.

The fact that for Poe a poem had to be the expression of a single mood—it would here be too long an excursis to try to demonstrate that *The Bells*, as a deliberate exercise in several moods, is as much a poem of one mood as any of Poe's—this fact can better be understood as a manifestation of a more fundamental weakness. Here, what I have to say I put forward only tentatively: but it is a view which I should like to launch in order to see what becomes of it. My account may go to explain, also, why the work of Poe has for many readers appealed at a particular phase of their growth, at the period of life when they were just emerging from childhood. That Poe had a powerful intellect is undeniable: but it seems to me the intellect of a highly gifted young person before puberty. The forms which his lively curiosity takes are those in which a pre-adolescent mentality delights: wonders of nature and of mechanics and of the supernatural, cryptograms and cyphers, puzzles and labyrinths, mechanical chess-players and wild flights of speculation. The variety and ardour of his curiosity delight and dazzle; yet in the end the eccentricity and lack of coherence of his interests tire. There is just that lacking which gives dignity to the mature man: a consistent view of life. An attitude can be mature and consistent, and yet be highly sceptical: but Poe was no sceptic. He appears to yield himself completely to the idea of the moment: the effect is, that all of his ideas seem to be *entertained* rather than believed. What is lacking is not brain power, but that maturity of intellect which comes only with the maturing of the man as a whole, the development and coordination of his various emotions. I am not concerned with any possible psychological or pathological explanation: it is enough for my purpose to record that the work of Poe is such as I should expect of a man of very exceptional mind and sensibility, whose emotional development has been in some respect arrested at an early age. His most vivid imaginative realizations are the realization of a dream: significantly, the ladies in his poems and tales are always ladies lost, or ladies vanishing before they can be embraced. Even in *The Haunted Palace*, where the subject appears to be his own weakness of alcoholism, the disaster has no moral significance; it is treated impersonally as an isolated phenomenon; it has not behind it the terrific force of such lines as those of François Villon when he speaks of his own fallen state.

Having said as much as this about Poe, I must proceed to inquire what it was that three great French poets found in his work to admire, which we have not found. We must first take account of the fact that none of these poets knew the English language very well. Baudelaire must have read a certain amount of English and American poetry: he certainly borrows from Gray, and apparently from Emerson. He was never familiar with England, and there is no reason to believe that he spoke the language at all well. As for Mallarmé, he taught English and there is convincing evidence of his imperfect knowledge, for he committed himself to writing a kind of guide to the use of the language. An examination of this curious treatise, and the strange phrases which he gives under the impression that they are familiar English proverbs, should dispel any rumour of Mallarmé's English scholarship. As for Valéry, I never heard him speak a word of English, even in England. I do not know what he had read in our language: Valéry's second language, the influence of which is perceptible in some of his verse, was Italian.

It is certainly possible, in reading something in a language imperfectly understood, for the reader to find what is not there; and when the reader is himself a man of genius, the foreign poem read may, by a happy accident, elicit something important from the depths of his own mind, which he attributes to what he reads. And it is true that in translating Poe's prose into French, Baudelaire effected a striking improvement: he transformed what is often a slipshod and a shoddy English prose into admirable French. Mallarmé, who translated a number of Poe's poems into French prose, effected a similar improvement: but on the other hand, the rhythms, in which we find so much of the originality of Poe, are lost. The evidence that the French overrated Poe because of their imperfect knowledge of English remains accordingly purely negative: we can venture no farther than saying that they were not disturbed by weaknesses of which we are very much aware. It does not account for their high opinion of Poe's *thought*, for the value which they attach to his philosophical and critical exercises. To understand that we must look elsewhere.

We must, at this point, avoid the error of assuming that Baudelaire, Mallarmé and Valéry all responded to Poe in exactly the same way. They are great poets, and they are each very different from the other; furthermore, they represent, as I have reminded you, three different generations. It is with Valéry that I am here chiefly concerned. I therefore say only that Baudelaire, to judge by his introduction to his translation of the tales and essays, was the most concerned with the personality of the man. With the accuracy of his portrait I am not concerned: the point is that in Poe, in his life, his isolation and his worldly failure, Baudelaire found the prototype of *le poète maudit*, the poet as the outcast of society—the type which was to realize itself, in different ways, in Verlaine and Rimbaud, the type of which Baudelaire saw himself as a distinguished example. This nineteenth-century archetype, *le poète maudit*, the rebel against society and against middle-class morality (a rebel who descends of course from the continental myth of the figure of Byron) corresponds to a particular social situation. But, in the course of an introduction which is primarily a sketch of the man Poe and his biography, Baudelaire lets fall one remark indicative of an aesthetic that brings us to Valéry:

'He believed [says Baudelaire], true poet that he was, that the goal of poetry is of the same nature as its principle, and that it should have nothing in view but itself.'

'A poem does not say something—it *is* something': that doctrine has been held in more recent times.

The interest for Mallarmé is rather in the technique of verse, though Poe's is, as Mallarmé recognizes, a kind of versification which does not lend itself to use in the French language. But when we come to Valéry, it is neither the man nor the poetry, but the *theory* of poetry, that engages his attention. In a very early letter to Mallarmé, written when he was a very young man, introducing himself to the elder poet, he says: 'I prize the theories of Poe, so profound and so insidiously learned; I believe in the omnipotence of rhythm, and especially in the suggestive phrase.' But I base my opinion, not primarily upon this credo of a very young man, but upon Valéry's subsequent theory and practice. In the same way that Valéry's poetry, and his essays on the art of poetry, are two aspects of the same interest of his mind and complement each other, so for Valéry the poetry of Poe is inseparable from Poe's poetic theories.

This brings me to the point of considering the meaning of the term 'la poésie pure': the French phrase has a connotation of discussion and argument which is not altogether rendered by the term 'pure poetry'.

All poetry may be said to start from the emotions experienced by human beings in their relations to themselves, to each other, to divine beings, and to the world about them; it is therefore concerned also with thought and action, which emotion brings about, and out of which emotion arises. But, at however primitive a stage of expression and appreciation, the function of poetry can never be simply to arouse these same emotions in the audience of the poet. You remember the account of Alexander's feast in the famous ode of Dryden. If the conqueror of Asia was actually transported with the violent emotions which the bard Timotheus, by skilfully varying his music, is said to have aroused in him, then the great Alexander was at the moment suffering from automatism induced by alcohol poisoning, and was in that state completely incapable of appreciating musical or poetic art. In the earliest poetry, or in the most rudimentary enjoyment of poetry, the attention of the listener is directed upon the subject matter; the effect of the poetic art is felt, without the listener being wholly conscious of this art. With the development of the consciousness of language, there is another stage, at which the auditor, who may by that time have become the reader, is aware of a double interest in a story for its own sake, and in the way in which it is told: that is to say, he becomes aware of style. Then we may take a delight in discrimination between the ways in which different poets will handle the same subject; an appreciation not merely of better or worse, but of differences between styles which are equally admired. At a third stage of development, the subject may recede to the background: instead of being the purpose of the poem, it becomes simply a necessary means for the realization of the poem. At this stage the reader or listener may become as nearly indifferent to the subject matter as the primitive listener was to the style. A complete unconsciousness or indifference to the style at the beginning, or to the subject matter at the end, would however take us outside of poetry altogether: for a complete unconsciousness of anything but subject matter would mean that for that listener poetry had not yet appeared; a complete unconsciousness of anything but style would mean that poetry had vanished.

This process of increasing self-consciousness—or, we may say, of increasing consciousness of language—has as its theoretical goal what we may call *la poésie pure*. I believe it to be a goal that can never be reached, because I think that poetry is only poetry so long as it preserves some 'impurity' in this sense: that is to say, so long as the subject matter is valued for its own sake. The Abbé Brémond, if I have understood him, maintains that while the element of *la poésie pure* is necessary to make a poem a poem, no poem can consist of *la poésie pure* solely. But what has happened in the case of Valéry is a change of attitude toward the subject matter. We must be careful to avoid saying that the subject matter becomes 'less important'. It has rather a different kind of importance: it is important as *means*: the *end* is the poem. The subject exists for the poem, not the poem for the subject. A poem may employ several subjects, combining them in a particular way; and it may be meaningless to ask 'What is the subject of the poem?' From the union of several subjects there appears, not another subject, but the poem.

Here I should like to point out the difference between a theory of poetry propounded by a student of aesthetics, and the same theory as held by a poet. It is one thing when it is simply an account of how the poet writes, without knowing it, and another thing when the poet himself writes consciously according to that theory. In affecting writing, the theory becomes a different thing from what it was merely as an explanation of how the poet writes. And Valéry was a poet who wrote very consciously and deliberately indeed: perhaps, at his best, not wholly under the guidance of theory; but his theorizing certainly affected the kind of poetry that he wrote. He was the most self-conscious of all poets.

To the extreme self-consciousness of Valéry must be added another trait: his extreme scepticism. It might be thought that such a man, without belief in anything which could be the subject of poetry, would find refuge in a doctrine of 'art for art's sake'. But Valéry was much too sceptical to believe even in art. It is significant, the number of times that he describes something he has written as an *ébauche*—a rough draft. He had ceased to believe in *ends*, and was only interested in *processes*. It often seems as if he had continued to write poetry, simply because he was interested in the introspective observation of himself engaged in writing it: one has only to read the several essays—sometimes indeed more exciting than his verse, because one suspects that he was more excited in writing them—in which he records his observations. There is a revealing remark in *Variété V*, the last of his books of collected papers: 'As for myself, who am, I confess, much more concerned with the formation or the fabrication of works [of art] than with the works themselves,' and, a little later in the same volume: 'In my opinion the most authentic philosophy is not in the objects of reflection, so much as in the very act of thought and its manipulation.'

Here we have, brought to their culmination by Valéry, two notions which can be traced back to Poe. There is first the doctrine, elicited from Poe by Baudelaire, which I have already quoted: 'A poem should have nothing in view but itself'; second the notion that the composition of a poem should be as conscious and deliberate as possible, that the poet should observe himself in the act of composition—and this, in a mind as sceptical as Valéry's, leads to the conclusion, so paradoxically inconsistent with the other, that the act of composition is more interesting than the poem which results from it.

First, there is the 'purity' of Poe's poetry. In the sense in which we speak of 'purity of language' Poe's poetry is very far from pure, for I have commented upon Poe's carelessness and unscrupulousness in the use of words. But in the sense of *la poésie pure*, that kind of purity came easily to Poe. The subject is little, the treatment is everything. He did not have to achieve purity by a process of purification, for his material was already tenuous. Second, there is that defect in Poe to which I alluded when I said that he did not appear to believe, but rather to entertain, theories. And here again, with Poe and Valéry, extremes meet, the immature mind playing with ideas because it had not developed to the point of convictions, and the very adult mind playing with ideas because it was too sceptical to hold convictions. It is by this contrast, I think, that we can account for Valéry's admiration for *Eureka*—that cosmological fantasy which makes no deep impression upon most of us, because we are aware of Poe's lack of qualification in philosophy, theology or natural science, but which Valéry, after Baudelaire, esteemed highly as a 'prose poem'. Finally, there is the astonishing result of Poe's analysis of the composition of *The Raven*. It does not matter whether *The Philosophy of Composition* is a hoax, or a piece of self-deception, or a more or less accurate record of Poe's calculations in writing the poem; what matters is that it suggested to Valéry a method and an occupation—that of observing himself write. Of course, a greater than Poe had already studied the poetic process. In the *Biographia Literaria* Coleridge is concerned primarily, of course, with the poetry of Wordsworth; and he did not pursue his philosophical enquiries concurrently with the writing of his poetry; but he does anticipate the question which fascinated Valéry: 'What am I doing when I write a poem?' Yet Poe's *Philosophy of Composition* is a *mise au point* of the question which gives it capital importance in relation to this process which ends with Valéry. For the penetration of the poetic by the introspective critical activity is carried to the limit by Valéry, the limit at which the latter begins to destroy the former. M. Louis Bolle, in his admirable study of this poet, observes pertinently: 'This intellectual narcissism is not alien to the poet, even though he does not explain the whole of his work: "why not conceive as a work of art the production of a work of art?" '

Now, as I think I have already hinted, I believe that the *art poétique* of which we find the germ in Poe, and which bore fruit in the work of Valéry, has gone as far as it can go. I do not believe that this aesthetic can be of any help to later poets. What will take its place I do not know. An aesthetic which merely contradicted it would not do. To insist on the all-importance of subject-matter, to insist that the poet should be spontaneous and irreflective, that he should depend upon inspiration and neglect technique, would be a lapse from what is in any case a highly civilized attitude to a barbarous one. We should have to have an aesthetic which somehow comprehended and transcended that of Poe and Valéry.

This question does not greatly exercise my mind, since I think that the poet's theories should arise out of his practice rather than his practice out of his theories. But I recognize first that within this tradition from Poe to Valéry are some of those modern poems which I most admire and enjoy; second, I think that the tradition itself represents the most interesting development of poetic consciousness anywhere in that same hundred years; and finally I value this exploration of certain poetic possibilities for its own sake, as we believe that all possibilities should be explored. And I find that by trying to look at Poe through the eyes of Baudelaire, Mallarmé and most of all Valéry, I become more thoroughly convinced of his importance, of the importance of his *work* as a whole. And, as for the future: it is a tenable hypothesis that this advance of self-consciousness, the extreme awareness of and concern for language which we find in Valéry, is something which must ultimately break down, owing to an increasing strain against which the human mind and nerves will rebel; just as, it may be maintained, the indefinite elaboration of scientific discovery and invention, and of political and social machinery, may reach a point at which there will be an irresistible revulsion of humanity and a readiness to accept the most primitive hardships rather than carry any longer the burden of modern civilization. Upon that I hold no fixed opinion: I leave it to your consideration.

AMERICAN LITERATURE AND THE AMERICAN LANGUAGE[1]

It is almost exactly forty-eight years ago that I made my first appearance on a public platform before a large audience. This was at the graduation exercises of the Class of 1905 of Smith Academy, an offshoot of this University; and my part in the ceremony was to deliver the valedictory poem of the year. I was informed afterwards, by one of my teachers, that the poem itself was excellent, as such poems go, but that my delivery was very bad indeed. Since then I have made some progress in elocution, and I have been more often criticized for the content of my speeches than for my manner of delivery; but I knew that today I should experience something like the trepidation which I well remember feeling on that evening so long ago. When I sat down to prepare my notes for this address, I found myself distracted by so many memories of my early years, that I was tempted either to talk about nothing else, or to pass them all over in silence. The first alternative would have produced something too personal and autobiographic for the dignity of this occasion; the second would have meant the suppression of feelings which I do not wish to suppress. I shall therefore, before proceeding to my subject, say something to indicate what it means to me to be here in St. Louis and to be speaking at Washington University in the hundredth year since its foundation; and I trust that a preamble somewhat longer than usual will not be amiss.

It is the fact that this is the centennial year of the University that gives me the excuse, as well as the stronger urge, to allude to my own upbringing. The early history of this University which

[1] An address delivered at Washington University, St. Louis, Missouri, on June 9th, 1953.

my grandfather served with tireless devotion until his death, is inextricably involved for me in family and personal history. I never knew my grandfather: he died a year before my birth. But I was brought up to be very much aware of him: so much so, that as a child I thought of him as still the head of the family—a ruler for whom *in absentia* my grandmother stood as vicegerent. The standard of conduct was that which my grandfather had set; our moral judgments, our decisions between duty and self-indulgence, were taken as if, like Moses, he had brought down the tables of the Law, any deviation from which would be sinful. Not the least of these laws, which included injunctions still more than prohibitions, was the law of Public Service: it is no doubt owing to the impress of this law upon my infant mind that, like other members of my family, I have felt, ever since I passed beyond my early irresponsible years, an uncomfortable and very inconvenient obligation to serve upon committees. This original Law of Public Service operated especially in three areas: the Church, the City, and the University. The Church meant, for us, the Unitarian Church of the Messiah, then situated in Locust Street, a few blocks west of my father's house and my grandmother's house; the City was St. Louis—the utmost outskirts of which touched on Forest Park, terminus of the Olive Street streetcars, and to me, as a child, the beginning of the Wild West; the University was Washington University, then housed in a modest building in lower Washington Avenue. These were the symbols of Religion, the Community and Education: and I think it is a very good beginning for any child, to be brought up to reverence such institutions, and to be taught that personal and selfish aims should be subordinated to the general good which they represent.

Unlike my father, my uncles, my brother, and several of my cousins, I was never enrolled as an undergraduate in Washington University, but was sent to another institution with which also there were family associations. But the earlier part—and I believe, the most important part—of my education is what I received in that preparatory department of the University which was named Smith Academy. My memories of Smith Academy are on the whole happy ones; and when, many years ago, I learned that the school had come to an end, I felt that a link with the past had been painfully broken. It was a good school. There one was taught, as is now increasingly rare everywhere, what I consider the essentials: Latin and Greek, together with Greek and Roman history, English and American history, elementary mathematics, French and German. Also English! I am happy to remember that in those days English composition was still called *Rhetoric.* Lest you infer that the curriculum was incredibly primitive, I will add that there was a laboratory, in which physical and chemical experiments were performed successfully by the more adroit. As I failed to pass my entrance examination in physics, you will not be surprised that I have forgotten the name of the master who taught it. But I remember other names of good teachers, my gratitude to whom I take this opportunity of recording: Mr. Jackson in Latin, Mr. Robinson in Greek, Mr. Rowe–though I was not one of his good pupils–in mathematics, Madame Jouvet-Kauffmann and Miss Chandler in French and German respectively. Mr. Hatch, who taught English, commended warmly my first poem, written as a class exercise, at the same time asking me suspiciously if I had had any help in writing it. Mr. Jeffries I think taught modern history; our ancient history was taught by the Greek and Latin masters. Well! so far as I am educated, I must pay my first tribute to Smith Academy; if I had not been well taught there, I should have been unable to profit elsewhere. And so far as I am badly educated, that is attributable to laziness and caprice. And before passing from the subject of Smith Academy, I wish to say that I remember it as a good school also because of the boys who were there with me: it seems to me that, for a school of small numbers, we were a well-mixed variety of local types.

Many other memories have invaded my mind, since I received the invitation to speak to you today; but I think these are enough to serve as a token of my thoughts and feelings. I am very well satisfied with having been born in St. Louis: in fact I think I was fortunate to have been born here, rather than in Boston, or New York, or London.

AMERICAN LITERATURE AND LANGUAGE

The title I have chosen for this address seems to indicate that I have two subjects. Why am I talking about both: 'American literature', and 'the American language'? First, because they are related, and second because they must be distinguished. It is profitable to clear our minds about the meaning of the term 'the American language' before proceeding to talk of American literature. As I have a reputation for affecting pedantic precision, a reputation I should not like to lose, I will add that I shall not ask 'what is literature?' However various may be people's notions as to what printed matter is literature and what is not, such differences of taste and judgment do not affect my problem.

My attention was recently called to this question of the differences between the English and the American language, on receiving a copy of a new American dictionary. It appeared to me an excellent dictionary of its size, and likely to be useful in England as well as in this country; and to those interested in the making of dictionaries and the problems arising in the definition of words, I commend also a pamphlet by one of the editors, Mr. David B. Guralnik, which struck me as very sound sense. But I was puzzled by the sub-title: it is called a dictionary 'of the American language'. Perhaps I am unconsciously bi-lingual, so that whichever language I hear or read seems to me my own; but certainly the vast majority of the words in this dictionary are words belonging to both America and England, and having the same meaning in both. And the definitions seemed to me to be written in English too. True, the spelling, where English and American usage differ, was the American spelling: but this presents no difficulty in England, where various editions of the work of Noah Webster (a famous lexicographer who I believe married my great-aunt) are in current use. And about spelling, I do not believe in hard and fast rules, and least of all in the hard and fast rules of champions of simplified spelling, such as the late Bernard Shaw. I hold that a word is something more than the noise it makes: it is also the way it looks on the page. I am averse to simplified spelling which destroys all traces of a word's origin and history. But I think, for example, that the English would do well to omit, from a word like 'labour', the superfluous U, which appears to be merely an etymological error. As to whether 'centre' should be spelt 'centre' or 'center', that seems to me a matter of indifference. There is much to be said for the American spelling 'catalog'; on the other hand I distrust simplifications of spelling that tend to alter pronunciation, as, for example, the shortening of 'programme' to 'program', which throws the stress onto the first syllable. And I think that the advocates of a systematic simplified spelling–such as those who recently introduced a Bill in Parliament–overlook the fact that in attempting to fix spelling phonetically, they are also attempting to fix pronunciation: and both pronunciation and spelling, in both England and America, must inevitably change from age to age under the pressure of usage and convenience.

Apart from the differences of spelling and pronunciation, the only other important difference which I discovered between this dictionary and the standard dictionaries in England, is that a number of words are included, which have not yet found their way into the latter. I was gratified, for instance, to find *grifter* and *shill*, two words which I first encountered in a fascinating book about one specialized area of the American vocabulary, called *The Big Con*. And about such words as *grifter* and *shill* I am willing to risk a prediction. Either they will disappear from the American vocabulary, to be replaced by newer and shinier words with the same meaning, or, if they become permanently settled, as Dr. Guralnik expects, they will find their way into the English vocabulary as well, and eventually into a supplement to the great Oxford dictionary. They will first appear in the vocabulary of that very large section of British society whose speech is constantly enriched from the films, and will make their way through the tabloid press to *The Times*, in *The Times* proceeding from the levity of the fourth editorial article to the solemnity of the first editorial article; and so their dictionary status in Britain will be assured. Many new words, of course, are ephemeral; and as Dr. Guralnik, in the essay to which I have referred, ruefully admits, a lexicographer may make the mistake of admitting a word to his dictionary just as it is on the point of going out of fashion: a mistake not unlike that of buying shares in a company just before its compulsory liquidation. Words can even disappear, and come into currency again after a period of seclusion. When I was a small boy, in this city, I was reproved by my family for using the vulgar phrase 'O.K.'. Then there was a period during which it seemed to have expired; but at some subsequent date it came to life again, and twenty-odd years ago swept like a tidal wave over England, to establish itself in English speech. As for its respectability here, I hold the most convincing piece of evidence yet: it occurs in a cable I received from Professor Cardwell.

Apart from some differences of spelling, pronunciation and vocabulary, there are between English and American a number of differences of idiom, for the most part reciprocally intelligible; there are also a few dangerous idioms, the same phrases with totally different meanings–in some cases leading to awkward misunderstanding and embarrassment. The sum total of these differences, however, does not seem to me to go so far as to justify us in speaking of English and American as different languages; the differences are no greater than between English as spoken in England and as spoken in Ireland, and negligible compared to the difference between English and Lowland Scots. But we must carry the question further, and ask: is it probable that speech in England and speech in America are developing in such a way that we can predict the eventual division into two languages, so distinct that each country will provide one more foreign language for the school curriculum of the other?

Perhaps we can draw some conclusions from the transformations of languages in the past. The obvious examples, of course, are the decline of Latin and its transmutation into the several Romance languages; and the development from Sanskrit, through Pali, of the modern Indian languages Bengali, Mahratti and Gujarati. I make no pretence of being a philologist; but even to a person untrained in that science there is a striking parallel between the relation of Italian to Latin, and the relation of Pali to Sanskrit. It would at first sight seem within the bounds of possibility, that in the course of time American speech and writing might come to differ as much from present-day English, as Italian and Bengali differ from Latin and Sanskrit.

The question has, of course, no bearing on the literature of today; and far from presenting a pleasing prospect to a living author, it is one which he must shudder to contemplate. Even if we refrain from calling our works 'immortal', we all of us like to believe that what we write will go on being read for a very long time indeed. We cannot relish the thought that our poems and plays and novels will, at best, be preserved only in texts heavily annotated by learned scholars, who will dispute the meaning of many passages and will be completely in the dark as to how our beautiful lines should be pronounced. Most of us, we know, have a pretty good chance of oblivion anyway; but to those of us who succeed in dying in advance of our reputations, the assurance of a time when our writings will only be grappled with by two or three graduate students in Middle Anglo-American 42 B is very distasteful. As it would not have pleased a late Latin poet in Southern Gaul to be told by a soothsayer that his language, over which he took so much trouble, would in a few centuries be replaced by something more up-to-date.

We must also face the possibility, if we can draw any conclusions from the metamorphosis of Latin, of a long period of time during which everything written in our language will be arid, pedantic and imitative. It is, of course, a necessary condition for the continuance of a literature, that the language should be in constant change. If it is changing it is alive; and if it does not change, then new writers have no escape from imitating classics of their literature without hope of producing anything so good. But when a change occurs such as that which led to the supersession of Latin by French, Italian, Spanish and Portuguese, the new languages have to grow up from the roots of the old, that is, from the common speech of uneducated people, and for a long time will be crude and capable of expressing only a narrow range of simple thoughts and feelings. The old culture had to decline, before the new cultures could develop. And for the development of a new and crude language into a great language, how much is not due to the happy accident of a few writers of great genius, such as Dante or Shakespeare?

Is the parallel with Latin and Sanskrit, however, valid? Is such a transformation, for better or worse, of English into two distinct languages on the two sides of the Atlantic likely to take place? I think that the circumstances nowadays are very different. If such a transformation should occur, it will be due to social, political and economic changes very different from anything that is happening now, and on such a vast scale that we cannot even imagine them. There is, I suspect, behind the thinking of such students of language as Mr. Mencken (whose monumental book on the American language is a philologist's picnic) a mistaken assimilation of language to politics. Such prophets seem to be issuing a kind of linguistic Declaration of Independence, an act of emancipation of American from English. But these patriotic spirits may be overlooking the other side of the picture.

In October last occurred an event which, while not as spectacular as the descent of Col. Lindbergh at Le Bourget in 'The Spirit of St. Louis', is equally remarkable in its kind. For the first time, apparently, an American robin, well named *Turdus migratorius*, crossed the Atlantic under its own power, 'favoured' according to the report, by 'a period of strong westerly weather'. This enterprising bird was also intelligent, for it chose to alight on Lundy Island, off the coast of Devon, which happens to be a bird sanctuary. Of course even birds, nowadays, are not allowed to travel without undergoing official inquisition, so our robin was trapped, photographed, and released; and, I hope, provided with a ration book. It is interesting to speculate on the future of this pilgrim. Either he (or she, for the sex is not stated) will be followed by another of the opposite sex, in which event we may expect that England will soon be populated by American robins; or else our lone pioneer must make the best of it, and breed with the English thrush, who is not *migratorius* but *musicus*. In the latter event, the English must look out for a new species of thrush, with a faint red spot on the male breast in springtime; a species which, being a blend of *migratorius* and *musicus*, should become known as the troubadour-bird, or organ-grinder.

Now, if the American robin can perform such feats, what cannot the American language do? Favoured by very strong westerly weather, of course. Unless you yourselves draw a linguistic iron curtain (and I think Hollywood, to say nothing of the proprietors of *Time*, *Life*, *The New Yorker* and other periodicals, would object to that) you cannot keep the American language out of England. However fast the American language moves, there will be always behind it the pattering of feet: the feet of the great British public eager for a new word or phrase. The feet may sometimes be a long way behind, but they are tireless. In the long run, I don't see how you can keep the American language to yourselves. Britain is of course eager also to export, though baffled by tariff walls; but it seems that at present the current of language flows from west to east. The last war strengthened the flow in that direction; and people from Land's End to John o'Groats are nourished on American films, the speech of which they understand, I have been told, a good deal better than the American public understand that of British films. It may be, that this west-east current will be the stronger for a long time to come: but, whatever happens, I believe that there will always be a movement in one direction or the other. So that, against the influences towards the development of separate languages, there will always be other influences tending towards fusion.

It has seemed to me worth while to get this question of language out of the way before attempting to say what I mean by American Literature: as I believe that we are now justified in speaking of what has never, I think, been found before, two literatures in the same language.

When, however, I assert that the term 'American literature' has for me a clear and distinct meaning, I do not believe that this meaning is wholly definable; and I shall try to explain in what respect I think it is undesirable to try to define it. Like many other terms, the term 'American literature' has altered and developed its meaning in the course of time. It means something different for us today from what it could have meant a hundred years ago. It has much fuller meaning now than it could have had then. By this I do not mean that American literature of the nineteenth century is less deserving of the name than American literature of the twentieth. I mean that the phrase could not mean quite the same thing to the writers of a century ago that it means to us;

that it is only in retrospect that their Americanness is fully visible. At the beginning, to speak of 'American literature' would have been only to establish a geographical distinction: Jonathan Edwards could hardly have understood what the term means today. Early American literature, without the achievements of later writers, would merely be literature written in English by men born or living in America. Washington Irving is less distinctively American than Fenimore Cooper. I suspect that the Leatherstocking novels, to a contemporary English reader, must have appeared to depict, not a new and different society, but the adventures of English pioneers in new and undeveloped country; just as I suppose they still have, for English boys, much the same fascination as good tales of adventure of early life in British dominions and colonies anywhere. (Cooper has suffered, like Walter Scott, from being read in early youth, and by many people never read again: it remained for D. H. Lawrence, who discovered Cooper later in life, to write probably the most brilliant of critical essays on him.) The English reader of the day, certainly, would hardly have recognized in Natty Bumppo, a new kind of man: it is only in retrospect that such differences are visible.

The literature of nineteenth century New England, however, is patently marked by something more than the several personalities of its authors: it has its own particular *civilized* landscape and the ethos of a local society of English origin with its own distinct traits. It remains representative of New England, rather than of America: and Longfellow, Whittier, Bryant, Emerson, Thoreau—and even the last of the pure New Englanders, Robert Frost—yield more of themselves, I believe, to people of New England origin than to others; they have, in addition to their qualities of wider appeal, a peculiar nostalgic charm for New Englanders settled elsewhere. And as for the writer who to me is the greatest among them, Nathaniel Hawthorne, it seems to me that there is something in Hawthorne that can best be appreciated by the reader with Calvinism in his bones and witch-hanging (*not* witch-hunting) on his conscience. So the landmarks I have chosen for the identification of American literature are not found in New England. I am aware that my choice may appear arbitrary; but in making such wide generalizations one must always take the risk. The three authors of my choice are Poe, Whitman, and Mark Twain.

I must hasten to explain what I do *not* mean. I do not imply that these writers are necessarily greater than others whom I have mentioned or could mention. Nor am I suggesting that these three men were individually 'more American' than others. Nor am I suggesting that American literature today *derives* from these three. Nor am I assuming that from a study of these three writers one could arrive at a formula of Americanism in literature. What their common American characteristics may be, is something I should consider it folly to attempt to define; and in seeking for their common qualities, one might easily overlook the essence of each.

I wish to emphasize the point that I am not concerned, in making such a selection, with questions of *influence*. A comparison of Poe and Whitman is illuminating. Amongst American poets, it is undoubtedly Poe and Whitman who have enjoyed the highest reputation abroad, both in English-speaking lands and in countries where they are known in translation. What is remarkable about the posthumous history of Poe is the fact that his influence in France, on and through the intermediary of three great French poets, has been immense; and that his influence in America and in England has been negligible. I cannot think of any good poet, here or in England, who has been sensibly influenced by Poe–except perhaps Edward Lear. How is it that Poe can be chosen as a distinctively American author, when there is so little evidence that any American poet since Poe has written any differently than he would have written if Poe had never lived?

To Walt Whitman, on the other hand, a great influence on modern poetry has been attributed. I wonder if this has not been exaggerated. In this respect he reminds me of Gerard Manley Hopkins–a lesser poet than Whitman, but also a remarkable innovator in style. Whitman and Hopkins, I think, both found an idiom and a metric perfectly suited for what they had to say; and very doubtfully adaptable to what anyone else has to say. One reason why such writers as Whitman and Hopkins attract imitators, is that in their less inspired verse they tend—as a writer with a highly idiosyncratic idiom may be tempted to do—to imitate themselves; and it is a man's imitation of himself, rather than his best work, that is most catching and most easily imitated. A true disciple is impressed by what his master has to say, and *consequently* by his way of saying it; an imitator—I might say, a borrower—is impressed chiefly by the way the master said it. If he manages to mimic his master well enough, he may succeed even in disguising from himself the fact that he has nothing to say.

It is possible, on the other hand, that the influence of Mark Twain may prove to have been considerable. If so, it is for this reason: that Twain, at least in *Huckleberry Finn*, reveals himself to be one of those writers, of whom there are not a great many in any literature, who have discovered a new way of writing, valid not only for themselves but for others. I should place him, in this respect, even with Dryden and Swift, as one of those rare writers who have brought their language up to date, and in so doing, 'purified the dialect of the tribe'. In this respect I should put him above Hawthorne: though no finer a stylist, and in obvious ways a less profound explorer of the human soul. Superficially, Twain is equally local, strongly local. Yet the Salem of Hawthorne remains a town with a particular tradition, which could not be anywhere but where it is; whereas the Mississippi of Mark Twain is not only the river known to those who voyage on it or live beside it, but the universal river of human life—more universal, indeed, than the Congo of Joseph Conrad. For Twain's readers anywhere, the Mississippi is *the* river. There is in Twain, I think, a great unconscious depth, which gives to *Huckleberry Finn* this symbolic value: a symbolism all the more powerful for being uncalculated and unconscious.

Here we arrive at two characteristics which I think must be found together, in any author whom I should single out as one of the landmarks of a national literature: the strong local flavour combined with unconscious universality. We must not suppose that the former can always be identified on superficial examination. What is identifiably local about Poe? Apart from *The Gold Bug* and a few other prose pieces, there is little in the work of Poe that appears to be based on the landscapes and the types of human being that he knew. His favourite settings are imaginary romantic places: a Paris or a Venice which he had never visited. It is very puzzling; but then Poe remains an enigma, a stumbling-block for the critic. Perhaps Poe's local quality is due simply to the fact that he never had the opportunity to travel, and that when he wrote about Europe, it was a Europe with which he had no direct acquaintance. A cosmopolitan experience might have done Poe more harm than good; for cosmopolitanism can be the enemy of universality—it may dissipate attention in superficial familiarity with the streets, the cafés and some of the local dialect of a number of foreign capitals; whereas universality can never come except through writing about what one knows thoroughly. Dostoevski is none the less universal, for having stopped in Russia. Perhaps all that one can say of Poe is that his was a type of imagination that created its own dream world; that anyone's dream world is conditioned by the world in which he lives; and that the real world behind Poe's fancy was the world of the Baltimore and Richmond and Philadelphia that he knew.

You will have noticed that the three authors on whom I am concentrating my attention are three of those who have enjoyed the greatest reputation abroad. It is possible for foreigners to be mistaken about contemporary writers: I know that the contemporary English estimate of the importance of some French writer, or the contemporary French estimate of the importance of some English writer, can be grotesque. But I think that when enough time has elapsed the continued appreciation of foreigners is likely to indicate that an author does combine the local with the universal. The foreigner may at first be attracted by the differences: an author is found interesting because he is so unlike anything in the foreigner's own literature. But a vogue due to novel differences will soon fade out; it will not survive unless the foreign reader recognizes, perhaps unconsciously, identity as well as difference. When we read a novel of Dostoevski, or see a play by Tchehov, for the first time, I think that we are fascinated by the odd way in which Russians behave; later, we come to recognize that theirs is merely an odd way of expressing thoughts and feelings which we all share. And, though it is only too easy for a writer to be local without being universal, I doubt whether a poet or novelist can be universal without being local too. Who could be more Greek than Odysseus? Or more German than Faust? Or more Spanish than Don Quixote? Or more American than Huck Finn? Yet each one of them is a kind of archetype in the mythology of all men everywhere.

Having got to this point, let me now suggest that a national literature comes to consciousness at the stage at which any young writer must be aware of several generations of writers behind him, in his own country and language, and amongst these generations several writers generally acknowledged to be of the great. The importance of this background for the young writer is incalculable. It is not necessary that this background should provide him with models for imitation. The young writer, certainly, should not be consciously bending his talent to conform to any supposed American or other tradition. The writers of the past, especially of the immediate past, in one's own place and language may be valuable to the young writer simply as something definite to rebel against. He will recognize the common ancestry: but he needn't necessarily *like* his relatives. For models to imitate, or for styles from which to learn, he may often more profitably go to writers of another country and another language, or of a remoter age. Some of my strongest impulse to original development, in early years, has come from thinking: 'here is a man who has said something, long ago or in another language, which somehow corresponds to what I want to say now; let me see if I can't do what he has done, in my own language—in the language of my own place and time.'

Such considerations should put us all on guard against an attitude of narrow national pride in our literature. Especially against asking questions such as 'is this new writer truly American or not? Does his work conform to the standards of America, to our definitions of what constitutes Americanism in literature?' It is obvious that such a critical censorship could only stifle originality. The cry has so often been raised about new writers: 'This isn't English!' or 'this isn't French!' or whatever the language may be. Also, there is always the danger of overvaluing the local product just because it is local; and of unconsciously judging our own writers by less exacting standards than those we apply to writers of other nations. We are, in every country, always exposed to that danger. And to narrow your admission to subject matter or to style already accepted, would be to affirm that what is American has been settled once for all. A living literature is always in process of change; contemporaneous living literatures are always, through one or more authors, changing each other; and the literature written in America in future generations will, you may be sure, render obsolete any formulations of 'what is American' based on the work of writers up to and including those now writing.

From time to time there occurs some revolution, or sudden mutation of form and content in literature. Then, some way of writing which has been practised for a generation or more, is found by a few people to be out of date, and no longer to respond to contemporary modes of thought, feeling and speech. A new kind of writing appears, to be greeted at first with disdain and derision; we hear that the tradition has been flouted, and that chaos has come. After a time it appears that the new way of writing is not destructive but re-creative. It is not that we have repudiated the past, as the obstinate enemies–and also the stupidest supporters–of any new movement like to believe; but that we have enlarged our conception of the past; and that in the light of what is new we see the past in a new pattern. We might now consider such a revolution as that which has taken place in poetry, both in England and in America, during the last forty years.

In talking about such an event, one must mention names. So, in order to be quite fair, I explain that I choose names as typical illustrations, that the poets mentioned are not necessarily valued in the order in which their names will occur, and that they are not all necessarily superior to all of the poets who are not mentioned. Furthermore, in any such literary revolution there is an overlap: some of the poets who continue to write in what is usually called a 'more traditional' manner are first-rate in their kind, and by the verdict of history may prove to be more highly prized than many of the poets who have written in newer ways.

In the first decade of the century the situation was unusual. I cannot think of a single living poet, in either England or America, then at the height of his powers, whose work was capable of pointing the way to a young poet conscious of the desire for a new idiom. It was the tail-end of the Victorian era. Our sympathies, I think, went out to those who are known as the English poets of the nineties, who were all, with one exception, dead. The exception was W. B. Yeats, who was younger, more robust, and of more temperate habits than the poets of the Rhymers' Club with whom he had associated in his youth. And Yeats himself had not found his personal speech; he was a late developer; when he emerged as a great modern poet, about 1917, we had already reached a point such that he appeared not as a precursor but as an elder and venerated contemporary. What the poets of the nineties had bequeathed to us besides the new tone of a few poems by Ernest Dowson, John Davidson and Arthur Symons, was the assurance that there was something to be learned from the French poets of the Symbolist Movement—and most of them were dead, too.

I do not propose to define the change that came about; I am merely tracing its course. Such a transformation as we have experienced in this century cannot be altogether attributed to one group of poets, still less to one individual. As so often happens in the fields of science, when a new discovery is made, it has been preceded by a number of scattered investigators who have happened to be groping, each at first in ignorance of the efforts of the others, in the same direction. In retrospect, it is often impossible to attribute the discovery to the genius of one scientist alone. The *point de repère* usually and conveniently taken, as the starting-point of modern poetry, is the group denominated 'imagists' in London about 1910. I was not there. It was an Anglo-American group: literary history has not settled the question, and perhaps never will, whether imagism itself, or the name for it, was invented by the American Ezra Pound or the Englishman T. E. Hulme. The poets in the group seem to have been drawn together by a common attraction towards modern poetry in French, and a common interest in exploring the possibilities of development through study of the poetry of other ages and languages. If imagism became more quickly and widely known in America than in England, that was largely because of the zealous, though sometimes misguided activity of Amy Lowell, who assumed the role of Advertising Manager for a movement which, on the whole, is chiefly important because of the stimulus it gave to later developments.

I think it is just to say that the pioneers of twentieth century poetry were more conspicuously the Americans than the English, both in number and in quality. Why this should have been must remain a matter for conjecture. I do not believe that it is attributable to the fact that so many more Britons were killed in the first war: the most remarkable of the British poets killed in that war whose work has been published, is in my opinion Isaac Rosenberg, who was outside the movement. Perhaps the young Americans of that age were less oppressed by the weight of the Victorian tradition, more open to new influences and more ready for experiment. (So far as my observation goes, I should say in general, of contemporary verse, that the most dangerous tendency of American versifiers is towards eccentricity and formlessness, whereas that of English versifiers is rather towards conventionality and reversion to the Victorian type.) But, looking at my own generation, the names that come immediately to mind are those of Ezra Pound, W. C. Williams, Wallace Stevens—and you may take pride in one who is a St. Louisan by birth: Miss Marianne Moore. Even of a somewhat younger generation, the names of Americans come to my mind most readily: Cummings, Hart Crane, Ransom, Tate. And I am choosing names only from among those whose work places them among the more radical experimenters: among poets of an intermediate type of technique the names of distinction are as numerous here as in England. And this is a new thing. In the nineteenth century, Poe and Whitman stand out as solitary international figures: in the last forty years, for the first time, there has been assembled a *body* of American poetry which has made its total impression in England and in Europe.

I am merely stating what seem to me cold facts. During the thirties the tide seemed to be turning the other way: the representative figure of that decade is W. H. Auden, though there are other British poets of the same generation whose best work will I believe prove equally permanent. Now, I do not know whether Auden is to be considered as an English or as an American poet: his career has been useful to me in providing me with an answer to the same question when asked about myself, for I can say: 'whichever Auden is, I suppose I must be the other'. Today there are several interesting younger poets in both countries, and England has acquired some valuable recruits from Wales. But my point in making this hurried review is simply this. In my time, there have been influences in both directions, and I think, to the mutual profit of literature on both sides of the Atlantic. But English and American poetry do not in consequence tend to become merged into one common international type, even though the poetry of today on one side of the ocean may show a closer kinship with poetry on the other side, than either does with that of an earlier generation. I do not think that a satisfactory statement of what constitutes the difference between an English and an American 'tradition' in poetry could be arrived at: because the moment you produce your definition, and the neater the definition is, the more surely some poet will turn up who doesn't fit into it at all, but who is nevertheless definitely either English or American. And the tradition itself, as I have said long ago, is altered by every new writer of genius. The difference will remain undefined, but it will remain; and this is I think as it should be: for it is because they are different that English poetry and American poetry can help each other, and contribute towards the endless renovation of both.

Dylan T.

THE AIMS OF EDUCATION[1]

1. *Can 'Education' be Defined?*

A well-known divine, in a recent volume[2] devoted to the sort of problems with which I shall be here concerned, has pronounced a judgment which I have tried to take to heart. 'It is', he says, 'unfortunately true that most educators do not sufficiently ignore literary dabblers but are, rather, unduly impressed by them.' He had preceded this harsh warning, to be sure, by a sentence which is less disturbing; he had just remarked: 'If the physical scientists, the religionists, the naturalists, the artists, and the students of human contacts could unite to bestow upon them [i.e., the literary dabblers] the privilege of talking exclusively to one another, and could turn jointly to the reconsideration of what constitutes true education to the restoration of sound thinking based upon adequate experience, there would be less confusion of mind in educational circles and more of that mutually helpful cooperation which properly exists between those who, by various methods and by complementary avenues, are seeking the one Truth.' I am not sure whether, in the present context, I am to be regarded as an artist or as a literary dabbler. Between helpful contribution and ignorant interference there may be a very narrow line indeed; and I must accept the risk if I am to say anything at all.

Education is a subject on which we all feel that we have something to say. We have all been educated, more or less; and we have, most of us, complaints to make about the defects of our own education; and we all like to blame our educators, or the

[1] The text of lectures delivered at the University of Chicago in November 1950. Printed in *Measure* (December 1950, Spring, Summer and Fall, 1951).

[2] Bernard Iddings Bell, *Crisis in Education* (New York, McGraw-Hill Book Company, 1949).

system within which they were compelled to work, for our failure to educate ourselves. And the literary dabbler has sometimes dabbled in teaching as well. I have been a schoolmaster, at a grammar school for one term, and for a year at a school for little boys; for three years of my life I conducted an Adult Education class once a week; at one time I was an Assistant in Philosophy taking weekly tutorial groups, and at a much later age I was responsible for a course for undergraduates in the subject—God forgive me—of Contemporary English Literature. I do not include the various series of public lectures which I have given at universities, because no one has to pass an examination on such lectures, and therefore they are no part of education. And I mention my nominal qualifications only to affirm that in my opinion they are, for my present task, no qualifications at all.

A couple of years ago I produced a book called *Notes towards the Definition of Culture*—a title which some readers declared to be pretentious and pedantic, and others declared to be evidence of mock-modesty. In this book I included, perhaps somewhat irrelevantly, a chapter treating a selection of what I believed to be current fallacies of educational theory. The chapter could not pretend to any unity or structure other than that of enumeration, and perhaps its chief function was to appease the feeling of irritation with a good deal of nonsense that had been talked and written in England during the war years. Having relieved the emotions with which my mind—or my liver—was charged, I felt much better; and thought that I should never be impelled to return to this subject. But, unfortunately, this chapter caught the eye of a very distinguished educator,[1] who, after a few polite commendations, exposed me publicly as the author of a mass of contradictions; and, in effect, called upon me to produce something more coherent or make my apology. Well, this is an attempt to do a little of both.

I immediately recognized one fault: that while, in the earlier and I hope better composed part of the book, I had attempted to distinguish between at least three different though closely related

[1] Robert M. Hutchins, 'T. S. Eliot on Education', *Measure*, I (Winter 1950).

meanings which the word *culture* has in different contexts, I had used the word *education* without bothering to analyse it in the same way. Yet it is immediately obvious that the word *education* means something different, to begin with when we are talking of what is offered and when we are talking of what is *received*; when we are talking of education as something done to people and when we mean what they do for themselves. We may mean the machine, or we may mean the contact of an apt pupil with the right teacher.

Here I must make an excursion. I have already exposed my willingness to risk the reputation of a literary dabbler in Education; I must risk that of a literary dabbler in semantics and semasiology. This is a still more forbidden preserve than Education; but the world is now so full of highly specialized subjects, the landscape is so completely divided into prohibited areas, with notice boards warning us that we must keep out, or that trespassers will be prosecuted, or simply to Beware of the Bull, that the literary dabbler is goaded to recklessness. So I shall mark off what I have to say on this subject—and abandon it later if it exposes me to too much derision—by entitling it 'Notes towards the Definition of Runcibility', or 'MacTaggart Refuted'.

The late John MacTaggart Ellis MacTaggart was a philosopher at Trinity College, Cambridge, who enjoyed a considerable reputation in his day. I have never read any of his works, but I believe that he was an Hegelian; an exponent of a philosophy now out of favour, except in the form of Dialectical Materialism. But it is said to have been Mr. MacTaggart who offered the explanation that the word *runcible* means *tortoise-shell*. He based this interpretation upon two loci, one in *The Owl and the Pussycat*, and the other in *The Pobble Who Has No Toes*. You will remember that the Owl and the Pussycat ate their wedding feast with a runcible spoon; and that the Pobble's Aunt Jobiska had a runcible cat with crimson whiskers. Recognizing that tortoise-shell spoons are sometimes made, and that tortoise-shell cats sometimes occur, MacTaggart affirmed that *tortoise-shell* was the only adjective applicable to both cats and spoons. Now, the question whether there is or is not any other adjective in the language applicable to both cats and spoons is one I do not raise: I am ready to accept MacTaggart's findings on this point. Nor do I rest my objection on his inadequate knowledge of the works of Edward Lear; I mean, on the fact that in another poem Lear describes himself as going forth 'in a runcible hat'. It would be easy for any disciple of MacTaggart to get round that with a footnote suggesting that Lear was an eccentric–which can hardly be denied–and that anyone like Lear might well have worn the shell of a tortoise as a hat: pointing out, incidentally, the similarity of shape between the shell of a tortoise and the academic headdress of doctors of letters at some English universities. No, I maintain that MacTaggart's method was wrong from the start.

It is a commonplace that the same word may develop two meanings which have no relation to each other except that of derivation from one root. Compare the verb *évincer* in French, meaning 'to eject, to dispossess', with the word *evince* in English, meaning nowadays 'to display, exhibit, manifest'. They both meant originally 'conquer'–they both started, that is, faithful to the meaning of the Latin from which they were formed. The modern use of the French verb is primarily legal. But the English verb has an interesting history. In the early sixteenth century, when it still meant 'overcome, prevail over', it meant also 'convince'–overcoming in argument (of course, 'convince' retains the significance of victory), and to 'confute'. A little later, it appears as 'constrain, extort'; at the same time it could mean 'establish' or 'vindicate'. Towards the end of the eighteenth century it appears to make a sudden leap into meaning 'to make evident or manifest.' This leap is not so puzzling as it might seem, when we look at the quotation illustrating this meaning in the Oxford English Dictionary, taken from the *Voyages of Captain Cook* (1790): 'Their pacific disposition is thoroughly evinced, from their friendly reception of all strangers'. Here the meaning of 1790, 'to make evident or manifest', is not very remote from one meaning of 1610: 'to prove by argument or evidence'. And 'to make evident or manifest' gives an easy transition to the use from the early nineteenth century to the present day, that of 'display, exhibit, manifest'. Thus, the transition of a word from one meaning to another may be easy, natural, and certainly in the history of *evince*, reasonable; each transition may be so imperceptible that the authors—and, we must not forget, the unremembered speakers—responsible for it may be unaware that they are committing any novelty: and yet it is a long way from the Latin verb *evincere*, to conquer, and the English verbs *exhibit* or *manifest*, which come from different roots. And there is a wide gulf between the meaning today of the English *evince* and the French *évincer*.

There is an obvious utility in acquainting ourselves with the history of important words, because without this understanding we are always reading modern meanings into the older texts of English literature. It is as necessary as it is to know, for example, that *suspenders* in England hold up socks, and that in America they support *pants*, which are held up in England by *braces*, and are not called *pants*, because that term is reserved for the garment underneath the American pants. But besides the variations of meaning of the same word in the same place at different times, and at the same time in different places, there is the still more important variation of meaning of the same word at the same time in the same place. Before proceeding farther, I want to suggest that this wobbliness of words is not something to be deplored. We should not try to pin a word down to one meaning, which it should have at all times, in all places, and for everybody. Of course there must be many words in a language which are relatively at least fixed always to one meaning. To say nothing of scientific terms, there are many substantives which name concrete objects and must have meant essentially the same thing throughout the history of the language: such as those two words which used to be employed by philosophers when they were considering whether anything existed or not—namely, *table* and *chair*. But there are also many words which *must* change their meaning, because it is their changes in meaning that keep a language *alive*, or rather, that indicate that the language *is* alive. If they did not change, it would mean either that we were living exactly the same life as our ancestors (the rate of change in the meanings of words in the language of a primitive tribe I should expect, other things being equal, to be very slow) or else that our language was no longer adequate to our needs—in which case, the more progressive language of some neighbour might supplant it.

Related to the change of meaning of words from one generation to another, are the variations of meaning which they may come to have at the same time, and it is these variations with which I am here concerned. When two words from the same root have acquired such diverse meanings in two different languages as *évincer* and *evince*, they are virtually two different words. The confusion would be intolerable if *evince* in English meant *both* 'to dispossess' and 'to manifest'. But there are many words which we must use in slightly different senses in different contexts; and the difference in meaning, though slight, may be very important. A great many of our confusions in thought arise from our not observing that we are using the same word in several senses.

Now to come back for a moment to the word *runcible*. It is a nonsense word, but I think we can learn something about 'sense words' from examining nonsense words. Lewis Carroll's 'portmanteau' words, like *slithy*, *gimble*, and *wabe*, are not pure nonsense words, for he defined their meaning: neither is Edward Lear's *spongetaneous*. But *runcible*, so far as I can discover, is a pure nonsense word: being such, it has no root. It cannot be defined. But I should deny that there was no relationship between his three uses of the same word. The rightness of the word, in each of these uses, the fact that it satisfies us as applicable to objects so different as a cat, a spoon, and a hat, is something that our sensibility acknowledges: we also feel that in each use there is a different shade of meaning. It is the nonsense shadow of the kind of word with which I am concerned, and so it cannot mean *tortoise-shell*. And incidentally, Lear was a poet; so, if he had meant *tortoise-shell*, he would probably have said *tortoise-shell*.

The word I am after, of course, is *education*. In the book in which I indiscreetly committed myself to a chapter of notes on education, I made, as I have just said, some effort to distinguish three senses in which we use the word *culture*: meaning something a little different when we are speaking of the individual, the group, or the society as a whole. I maintained that it would not do to have three different words, or even to say always 'culture A, B or C', because these meanings interpenetrate each other and give significance to each other; but that we must be constantly on guard not to make statements about one category which are applicable only to another. It is possible that I have done so myself, even in chapters in which I was trying to distinguish. We can hardly avoid occasionally misleading our readers, for it is more than we can do always to avoid misleading ourselves. And we must remember that the meaning of a word is never wholly represented by its definition, that is, by other words; and that there is an implicit unity between all the meanings of a word like 'culture' which cannot be wholly confined within a definition: this is the unity which we feel in going through the several definitions of the word in current use.

What I did not do, however, was to analyse the several meanings of 'education'. I do not think that any of the authors whose statements I was calling into question had done so either; but that is no excuse. Like the authors whom I criticized, I let it be assumed that 'education' had one meaning only.

Some light on the complexity of the meaning of the word can be found by examining, as we did with *evince*, the history of the word. I return to the O.E.D. The word *education* follows a pretty straight course, except for including the training of animals, and for one technical application to the training of silkworms. It is first applied to the teaching of the very young: in fact, the first illustration given, dating from 1540, speaks of the education of infants one year old. It then proceeds to the training of young persons with reference to the station they are to occupy in life: that is, to the fixed group. (Early treatises on education, of course, were concerned with preparing young gentlemen for life at court.) It proceeds next to 'the systematic instruction, schooling or training given to the young in preparation for the work of life'; also 'the whole course of scholastic instruction which a person has received': that is to say, the word develops along with schools and colleges; but it still has frequently a professional connotation—legal, for example, or medical. Finally, it becomes 'culture, or development of powers, formation of character, as contrasted with the imparting of mere knowledge or skill'. And it is at this stage that we begin to get into difficulties over the meaning of the word in different contexts.

As time goes on, and a language ages, it becomes more difficult to find out what words mean, and whether they are meaning the same thing to different people. And when we use the *word* 'education', we are probably using it either so comprehensively that in consequence of meaning everything, it denotes nothing, or else we have at the back of our minds one particular meaning. We may, for instance, be thinking of the 'educated man'. But the highest type of educated man is not simply a man who has been through the best educational institutions; he is, to begin with, more educable than most, and is one who has done much to educate himself since he ceased to be a pupil. We may mean by the educated man, one who is very highly trained and highly proficient in some very narrow specialty; or we may mean a man who has had a good 'all-round education'—which we then may proceed to sketch out, though we seldom agree as to what education is all-round, admitting that no one person has the time, even if he has the capacities, to be educated 'all-round'. When we think of the individual, we are apt, I believe, and rightly, to be stressing what the man does for himself, rather than what is done to him. And the perfectly educated man, like the perfectly cultured man, does not exist; and the kind of perfection in question differs according to the environment. It is easier to think in terms of the group. In earlier times, of which there remain vestiges, it was the *social* group; in our time it is more importantly the technical group. So long as you are concerned merely with a small group of the same social rank, the question of the purpose or meaning of education hardly arises. For the fact that all of the pupils have much the same background, have nominally the same religious allegiance, and will proceed to later activities within the same group, means that a great deal of 'education' in the widest sense can be taken for granted or ignored. And where a technical education is concerned, its aim is clear, its success or failure can be measured; the only question is at what age to begin.

The students will, no doubt, come from very different backgrounds, and will eventually scatter, to lead, apart from their professional activities, very different lives; but the question of what they should be taught, and in what order, is a manageable one. The real difficulty arises when the word *education* is taken in its most recent meaning, 'culture, or development of powers, formation of character'. For the meaning in relation to a social or professional group is distinguished by all the things that it is not; whereas in the widest sense, education covers the whole of life for the whole of society.

I am not objecting to this developed meaning of the word. I think it was inevitable with the development of society in magnitude, in complexity, and in organization, and with the pressure so evident in our own time, towards the conscious direction and centralization of more and more of life. But we have been forced into meaning all this by education, in an age when, being more conscious of our culture, we are more doubtful of it; and in an age when there are divergent views as to how character should be formed. And there is the increasing danger, that in applying this definition to the purposes of our educational institutions, we expect them to do for society what society ought to do for itself. And 'culture, development of powers, formation of character', provide an especially hard task to be set before our educational institutions of the present day. These institutions are, in all countries, so vast; they bring together students of such different types; they have so many departments; they are at the same time so highly organized and so formless. We can easily aim at more, and accomplish less, than our grandparents and great-grandparents did.

I should like to return to the list of the three ends of education suggested by Dr. C. E. M. Joad, which I criticized briefly in my book, because they seem to me as good as any three that I have seen given. They are:

To enable a boy or girl to make his or her living.
To equip him to play his part as a citizen of a democracy.
To enable him to develop all the latent powers and faculties of his nature and so enjoy a good life.

These make up, in fact, the professional, the social, and the individual aspects of education, in the terms in which Dr. Joad sees them. The first, the training for a livelihood, is certainly a permanent part of education. But it is, of course, to be interpreted in connection with the second and third. The livelihood has to fit in with the needs and requirements of society; it has also to be the sort of living for which the individual is best fitted by tastes and capacities. What is implied is a good society: for it is well known that in most societies some highly important activities are underpaid or even discouraged. A good society, as well as a decent individual, is also implied by the third end, that of 'developing the latent powers'. For some of the latent powers might be evil, and the development of the individual's powers is not solely for his enjoyment of life: some of them should be beneficial, and the rest harmless to society.

So we get to the question, what sort of society should it be? I am not happy to say simply 'in a democracy' as do Dr. Joad and others. In the first place, this is a statement to which every politician nowadays in every country would subscribe; and when everybody agrees on using the same word to describe totally different institutions, it becomes suspect. In the second place, as the word always suggests to everybody the particular kind of democracy in which he lives, the next step is to say 'my democracy is more democratic than your democracy'; whereas it seems to me that each democratic country has to fashion a democracy which will differ in some respects from those of others, but may be equally 'democratic'. Next, a democracy worthy of the name seems to me a democracy of human beings, not simply of formal systems; much depends upon the citizens and those whom they choose to represent them. There may be a lack of accord between the formal institutions and the ethos of the particular people that operates them; and for this reason, and because of corruption amongst those who make politics a profession, or indifference or ignorance or prejudice or ill-regulated emotion amongst the public, a democracy can sometimes work very badly.

We all agree on the affirmation that a democracy is the best possible aim for society; and the widest definition of democracy that *I* can find, is a society in which the maximum of responsibility is combined with the maximum of individual liberty. But we cannot leave it at that. For one thing, the concept of 'responsibility' seems to imply that of freedom'; and vice versa. One becomes responsible not simply by having tasks imposed which one cannot escape; for an individual to be truly responsible he must be free to shirk his responsibilities; and no one can be said to be truly 'a free man' who is 'irresponsible'—that is, at the mercy of his whims or appetites—a man who takes no responsibility for himself.

I should make it quite clear that I accept Dr. Joad's assertion that one of the aims of education should be to equip its products to play their parts as citizens of a democracy. When I say I accept it, I mean that any other assertion which contradicted it *within the same area of discourse* would be false. Such an assertion would be, for instance, that 'one of the aims of education should be to equip its products to play their parts as citizens of an anti-democracy', or 'it is not the business of education to form good citizens'. What I want to recognize is simply, that a definition of one term is likely to involve the use of undefined defining terms. Now, this seems to be inevitable; it is a permanent condition of language and of thought. A definition is sufficient, when, for the purpose of using the defined term correctly, we do not need a further definition of the defining terms. It is inadequate and dangerous, when we extend the meaning of the defining terms to what was not in the intention of the definer—because there is always this limitation to a definition, that it is made by somebody, and is apprehended by somebody. There are areas of exact thought in which it does not matter who the definer was; but here we are not in one of those happy scientific paradises.

Now, in the assertion under examination, I think that it is necessary to assume that we mean the essence of democracy—that we are not selecting one meaning rather than another. It must mean all that I have suggested a few minutes ago: not merely a form of government, but a common ethos, a common way of responding emotionally, even common standards of conduct in private life. But the reader of such a definition is apt to respond to the word 'democracy' merely with a few shreds of impressions of conventions, elections, going to vote, and the like. If he proceeds to something more articulate, he may proceed to define democracy, either in a way that suggests to some readers that he doesn't mean democracy at all, or else in a way that leaves them unsatisfied. Dr. Edward Leen, an Irish theologian, in an interesting and commendable book *What is Education?*, says: 'It is agreed that a certain acceptable meaning can be given to the statement that youth must be educated for democracy, provided we are clear as to what democracy means.' He then goes on to tell us what he means. 'Democracy rightly understood,' he says, 'is nothing less than aristocracy.' He should, I think, have said 'aristocracy rightly understood', because he goes on to give his own meaning to 'aristocracy'. He means 'an aristocracy of worth, not an aristocracy of accident.' The admission to it, he says, is not by money or by birth, but by personal, moral, and intellectual effort.

Now for one thing, this is not the common meaning of 'aristocracy', and I am rather suspicious of attempts to change the common meaning by violence. But, for another, Dr. Leen has, it seems to me, merely pushed the problem a stage farther away without helping us to get there; for the problem of how to get the best men as rulers is one which remains to be solved. And furthermore, it does not seem to me ideally democratic, for it at least may suggest that society is sharply divisible into rulers and ruled; he has, it seems to me, limited his view of democracy to the political aspect.

It is beginning to appear that a formal definition of education, and a generalized statement of its purpose, is not to be easily come by. The statement 'to equip boys and girls to play their part in a democracy' is evidently only a secondary purpose, unless we choose to restrict very narrowly the meaning of 'education'. For it is obvious that if this is an essential part of education, many of the greatest sages and scholars of the past cannot be called educated; and we must say this even of the fathers of democracy. As a secondary purpose, it must be accepted only with full awareness of its limitations and dangers. The chief danger is that, in a democratic society, education may come to be interpreted as *educational adaptation to environment.* Surely, no one is educated to play his part in a democracy, if he has merely been adapted to the particular routine of democracy in which he finds himself; he must be educated to criticize his own democracy, to measure it against what democracy should be, and to recognize the differences between what is proper and workable in one democracy and what is proper and workable in another. He must be adapted to it, certainly: for without being adapted to it, he cannot play a part in it, he can hardly survive in it. But he must not be completely adapted to it in the form in which he finds it around him; for that would be to train a generation to be completely incapable of any change or improvement, unable to make discoveries or experiments, or to adapt itself to those changes which go on perpetually without anyone's having deliberately intended to bring them about. So 'education for democracy' is not so simple a matter as it sounds when we first hear it.

We have seen that 'training to earn a livelihood', which is one of the purposes of education, means training in a particular society: a livelihood is made in quite different ways in different societies, and even in the best societies some of the ways of making a livelihood are far from praiseworthy. And the third purpose of education, 'to enable us to develop all the latent powers and faculties of our nature and so enjoy a good life', also has its full meaning only within the bounds of a particular society. If we mean by 'a good life' the kind of life which that society considers good, we are committed to a programme of complete adaptation; if we mean by it, a good life independent of the social limitations of place and time, we must have some other standard of goodness. And the development of *all* our latent powers (even if we confine ourselves to powers for *good*) is limited by the livelihood we have to earn, and the society in which we earn it. So it would seem that education must be partly a process of adaptation to our society as it is; partly a preparation for the sort of society we want it to become; and at the same time we are aware that education, and our responsibility towards those we educate, are not comprehended by our conception of our society as it is, however modified by what we aspire that it should be. What education would we design, for instance, for an individual destined to become a permanent Robinson Crusoe? It would have to be pretty comprehensive, certainly, in practical skills: there is very little in the way of applied science that would come amiss; but his education would have to include, surely, some mental discipline, in the way of furnishing him with the mental and spiritual resources with which that hero was so well equipped, for enduring solitude. What education, on the other hand, would we design for pupils who we knew would have to live in a thoroughly *bad* society? Bad, not merely corrupt as all societies are, but organized towards evil? Our educators, fortunately, do not have to devise curricula for these situations; but unless our definition of education can give an answer to these two questions, it is not a complete definition.

I do not suggest that we ought to try to give a complete definition; I suggest only that it is well to recognize the incompleteness of any definition that we give. The meaning of a word like 'education' is, to begin with, more than the sum of the meanings given in the dictionary, meanings which are no more than an account of the uses to which a word has been put by writers throughout several centuries. But, when a language is alive, such words will constantly be used in new contexts; they acquire new associations and lose some of the old ones; and every great writer contributes something to the meaning of the key words which he uses, those which are characteristic of his personal style. Some of these uses of the word die with him, others enter into the common language. The process of enrichment of the meaning of a word cannot go on indefinitely, without some uses of it becoming obsolete and forgotten: partly because our minds cannot contain them all, even if we are acquainted with them through our study of literature, and partly because an indefinite extension of meaning would lead to ambiguity and confusion. It is one of the advantages of the study of a dead language that it is more manageable, that the words in it have come to the limit of their meaning: there they are in the texts, and their meaning can be no more than what the authors, during the time in which that language flourished, have given them. We do not want our language to become a dead language; yet we are always trying, and indeed must try, however vainly, if we are to think at all, to fix a permanent meaning for every word.

We all mean, by education, some training of the mind and generally of the body also—so that we can include training for sport as well as for skills directed to some further purpose. But we can have no clear or useful idea of what education is, unless we have some notion of what this training is *for*. Thus we come to inquire what is the purpose of education, and here we get deeply into the area of conflict. We can, as I have said, produce definitions which are valid within a limited but unstable context, as when we speak of 'training to play our parts as citizens of a democracy'. It is fortunate that there are areas of discourse within which we can agree that some of the words we use do not need to be defined, inasmuch as we are using the word in the same way—whatever that way is. But there is a point beyond which we become aware that the same proposition means something different to two people both accepting it—this happens very often in treaties and other political negotiations; and then we have to try to define one or more words which we had been employing under the impression that they meant the same thing to both of us. Just as a dogma may not have to be asserted until a heresy has appeared to provoke it, so a word may not need to be defined until we discover that two or more people are using it with a difference of meaning.

I do not suggest for a moment that we should abandon the attempt to define the purpose of education (and the definition of the purpose is an inevitable step from the definition of the word itself). If we see a new and mysterious machine, I think that the first question we ask is, 'What is that machine *for*?' and afterwards we ask, 'How does it do it?' But the moment we ask about the purpose of anything, we may be involving ourselves in asking about the purpose of everything. If we define education, we are led to ask 'What is Man?'; and if we define the purpose of education, we are committed to the question 'What is Man for?' Every definition of the purpose of education, therefore, implies some concealed, or rather implicit philosophy or theology.

In choosing one definition rather than another, we are attracted to the one because it fits in better with our answer to the question 'What is Man for?' We may not know what our own answer is, because it may not be fully conscious, and may be wholly unconscious; our answer is not always in our minds, but in the unconscious assumptions upon which we conduct the whole of our lives. The man who has made the definition which you accept or reject, wholly or in part, may be more aware or less aware of the implication of his definition than you are: at the moment when he makes the definition, and at the moment of your reaction to it, probably neither of you is aware of all that is beyond the margin of the field of discourse.

It might appear from what I have just been saying—if anything appears at all—that we ought to drop the question 'What is education for?' and proceed to the question 'What is Man for?' I do not know much about Man, but I am sure that our minds do not and cannot work in that way. We cannot discuss ultimate problems in a vacuum; the whole of our mind, sensibility, and experience of life must be brought to bear upon them; part of our experience has been obtained in dealing with these secondary problems in their more limited contexts; and it is these secondary problems which provide us with the reasons for attacking the primary ones. Furthermore, the secondary problem is more nearly and obviously related to the practical questions which arise every day, and which have to be dealt with immediately in some fashion if we are to carry on at all. Nor do I deplore the fact that so many and various accounts of the purpose of education are given. We must go on inventing new ones. Each answer is a clue to what education means to somebody; an incentive to finding out what it means for oneself. If it meant exactly the same thing to everybody, the world would be a very dead place indeed; so we have no reason to deplore the fact, if we find the meaning of education as elusive as the meaning of the word *runcible*.

THE AIMS OF EDUCATION

2. *The Interrelation of Aims*

So far, we have accepted as the most convenient starting point Dr. Joad's list of the three aims of education: the professional, or, in the humblest way of putting it, training to earn a living; the social, or, in Dr. Joad's way of putting it, preparation for citizenship; and the individual, or, in Matthew Arnold's way of putting it, the pursuit of perfection. But we cannot define education as merely the sum of these three activities; for if the term 'education' is to cover all three and not be wholly applicable to any one of them separately, we must appreciate some relationship, or rather some mutual implication, between them, such that each, while it may still be called education, is not the whole of education by itself. We recognize that the choice of a livelihood is limited, first, by the capacities of the individual; and second, by the kinds of activity favoured or discouraged by the society in which the individual finds himself, or in other words, the kinds of thing that people are prepared to pay a man to do. The choice of a livelihood involves some adaptation to the social milieu, although some men are willing to earn a very modest living in order to pursue a vocation which seems more worth while to them than it does to their neighbours. Furthermore, we observe that there are some ways of earning a living which are not in themselves commendable, and which we should not train people for: parasitical activities, which feed, at best, on the follies, and, at worst, on the vices of mankind. And this raises the question of moral criteria; so that the formula of earning a living is doubly inadequate, and we are led to both of the other aims on our list. Or, if we start from the formula 'training for citizenship', that implies training to make a living; or, in a wider sense (including those persons, a few of whom still exist, who are able to live on unearned income), training in some useful activity. We can stretch the term 'useful' very wide so as to include activities which to the great majority of mankind seem quite useless; but I think we must agree that the man who is, according to *every* standard of measurement, completely useless to society, is hardly a successful product of education. And I think we must agree that the best citizens are likely to be those who develop 'the latent powers and faculties of their nature'; or at least that any society which does not endeavour to make possible the development of the latent powers and faculties of those who have the best latent powers and faculties to develop has a very narrow and mediocre conception of citizenship, and will not be a society worth educating people for. Finally, the development of the latent powers and faculties depends upon the pursuit of the right activities, including the best occupation for a livelihood that the individual can find; and depends also upon the individual's finding himself in a society in which his powers and faculties can be nourished and can bear fruit. So each one of these aims of education leads to a process which can in the right context be called 'education', though we cannot define education by any one of them alone. And each one of these paths leads inevitably to moral judgments and decisions which take us beyond the limits within which we should like to confine 'education' if the subject is to be manageable.

The danger of the list, as a mere list, is that we cannot long retain all three of the items in equal balance in our minds, once we start trying to educate people. This is not only because, in consequence of attending to one, we are apt to overlook the others; it may be also that in practice the three aims happen sometimes to be incompatible, and we are forced to emphasize one rather than the other. And when we find we have gone too far to one extreme, the natural reaction is to go too far to the other.

When I first revisited universities, after the end of the war, I was told that the new generation—both of those whose higher education had been interrupted or deferred, and of those a few years younger coming straight from their schools—was much more serious than that which I had known in the thirties, and than that of undergraduates in my own time. I am speaking of universities in England, in America, and on the continent of Europe. And indeed, ocular evidence appeared to confirm this. On every quadrangle or campus, and in the streets of university towns, I saw earnest faces with concentrated expressions, of young people who seemed to be always in transit from lecture to lecture, from tutorial to their rooms, from their rooms to the library. It was suggested to me that the anxiety visible on every face was the anxiety about a future livelihood. They were anxious to learn, to learn as much as possible in the shortest time, in order to qualify themselves for the jobs which they were out to get as soon as they had their diplomas in their hands. Now it seems to me that in my time we were far less concerned, during the earlier academic years at least, with what we were going to do afterwards. There were, of course, the minority who, unlike myself, had revealed a distinct bent, in scholarship or in some particular field of science, and were so devoted to their subjects that they looked forward already to a higher degree and to a lifetime of teaching the subject of their interest. But I do not think that even these were oppressed by the thought that they might have any difficulty in getting a job: they might not find a very good place to start with, but the future was open. They looked forward rather to earning a livelihood through their mastery of the subject they were interested in; but not so many of them were concerned simply with taking a degree as a necessary condition of getting a job of some kind they knew not what.

Now I am aware that many of my contemporaries left college having gained only the advantage of being three or four years older when they came to look for a job than they would have been had they not gone there. One profited, of course, from friendships, from extra-curricular activities, and from associating with men of one's own generation from various parts of America. But I am not at the moment concerned with incidental benefits, but with the formal tuition. And on the wrong side of the balance sheet, I must put the unrestraint of the free elective system as practised in my time. By passing examinations in a certain number of wholly unrelated subjects one could, in three or four years, obtain the certificate of education—the diploma of bachelor of arts. The only limitation was that you could not follow two courses in the same year if their lecture hours coincided. I knew one man whose principle of choice of courses was that the lectures should all fall on Tuesdays and Thursdays, with no lecture on Saturday: thus, he was free to spend four days a week in New York. I should add that he did not follow even this course of study with sufficient application to qualify him for a degree, though he made a passing acquaintance with the appreciation of music, and with housing problems in mining communities. I am not, however, so much concerned with the effect of this system of education upon the idler, as with its effect upon the young man like myself, with a good deal of ill-regulated curiosity in out-of-the-way subjects, who took, for instance, a perverse pleasure in dabbling with late Latin and Greek authors without having mastered the real classics. It is not the system of education promoted by those educators of the late nineteenth century whose notions had been developed in Germany that I am defending; what I regret is the disappearance of a state of mind among undergraduates themselves. Those who were fundamentally serious minded, and not triflers, were able to pursue their studies for their own sake, simply because they cared for them. The change came from economic, social and perhaps political developments in the last forty years, which have been much accelerated in this decade; and, if conditions are the same today, one cannot urge students to abandon an attitude which has been forced upon them by circumstances. I only wish to make the point that while the three aims of education formulated by Dr. Joad are complementary to each other, they can also interfere with each other. This may become a little more intelligible if I suggest that the aim which a man sets before himself, in training himself to earn a living, and the aim he sets before himself, in working to develop and cultivate his mind and sensibility, are different in kind. The first is an aim in pursuing which you can keep consciously in mind both the end and the means. You decide on the general field in which you wish to find employment, and then follow the course of instruction laid down, or generally accepted as suitable preparation for that employment. But for that cultivation of powers and faculties which tends to make us educated men, apart from our professional occupations, disinterestedness is necessary: you have to pursue studies for their own sake, for the love of truth, or wisdom, or at least curiosity, ignoring any practical advantages which may come to you from mastering them.

Of course, I have oversimplified this problem. If a man is to excel in any profession, he must love the activity for its own sake; and its usefulness to society, and the financial and other rewards that it brings him, are merely justifications of it. Most of us, at least, find it necessary to persuade ourselves that the work we do is of some importance. But, on the other hand, the man who is narrowly concentrated in his own particular work is not wholly an educated man; he may be not only uncultivated, but in outside affairs an utter simpleton. Most of us have to sacrifice possibilities of educating ourselves beyond some point simply because we have not the time for it if we are to get our work done. On the other hand, the man who does not concentrate on work of his own, but pursues his education in various directions, will be only a dilettante. In the world there is room for both the narrow specialist and the dilettante. But the fact that there are different aptitudes and functions in a world in which we have to be tolerant of others does not solve the educational problem. And it seems to me that often, in our attempt to balance special training with general culture, we incline to methods of education which produce men and women highly trained in some narrow interest of science or scholarship, and smatterers in everything else; we tend to put them through a course of study which attempts to combine the technical institute with the young ladies' finishing school. For if 'training to earn a living' and the 'development of all the latent powers and faculties' are treated simply as two unrelated disciplines to which every pupil must be subjected, the latter will be no more than useful as a kind of recreation. When we see that we perform our specialized work all the more intelligently because of seeing it in relation to the work of all sorts of other people, living and dead, who have devoted themselves to quite other types of work than our own, we are on our way to solving for ourselves—this means finding the right compromise for ourselves—the puzzle of the balance between those activities in which we participate, and those of which we can only hope to be an appreciative spectator.

Perhaps I can give this discussion more appearance of reality, or at least provide light relief in the way of something more apprehensible, by asking 'What sort of education should a poet have?' I don't think any parents have ever brought a child up with a view to his becoming a poet; some parents have brought up their children to be criminals; but for good and loving parents a poet is almost the last thing they could want their child to be, unless they thought it was the only way of saving him from becoming a criminal. I suppose that poets, during their tender years, usually show an interest in language and expression, and give some indication of a bent for the study of languages rather than science. This is not always true; I have known men who in childhood seemed to their parents to give promise of becoming Humphry Davys or Clerk Maxwells, and suddenly shifted their interest to literature at fifteen or sixteen. Certainly, the fact that a child writes verses is no indication whatever that he will become a poet. Nearly everybody has written verses: a wise parent should not discourage the habit, but should attach no specific significance to it. But if the young poet is of the usual kind, he will probably excel in languages, particularly his own; and is likely to be of the type which flourishes on Latin and Greek. Certainly, the poet in later life ought to be equipped with a good knowledge of Latin and Greek literature, make himself fluent in one modern language besides his own, and have a reading knowledge of several others. How few of us, however, satisfy that qualification: I certainly do not. But what else should he study, from the point at which it is evident at least that a literary education is the most suitable for him? In the first place, he usually has to make his living, and poetry is conspicuously the occupation by which no one can expect to make a living. For most men, there is the conflict between the claims of the occupation which they make their chief concern in life, and the claims of 'the latent powers and faculties'. But the poet has a threefold problem to solve: he must earn a living, he must practise and perfect himself in writing, and he must cultivate other interests as well. He must do the last, not merely in order to exercise latent powers, in order to become a cultivated man; but because he must have these other interests in order to have something to write about. Almost no form of knowledge comes amiss (besides, of course, the knowledge of as much of the best poetry in several languages as he can assimilate) because without other intellectual interests his experience of men and women will be very limited. The condition is that everything should be grist that comes to his mill; that he should have a lively curiosity in what men have thought and done, and be interested in these things for their own sake. He is perpetually engaged in solving the problem that every man must solve for himself, that of relating every human activity to his own; and he cannot tell how much, or what, of the subjects he investigates will be directly useful to him as a poet. But his poetry will inevitably be affected by his studies and interests, and the more he can assimilate the better. And finally, he has the problem of procuring a livelihood: he has sometimes to choose between a dull routine which provides little or no food for his mind, or an active and interesting one which leaves him very little time and energy. For some, this livelihood can be found in various forms of journalistic or paraliterary occupation; in teaching and lecturing. For others, something as remote as possible from their literary interests is desirable: something which uses none of the kind of energy that goes into poetry, and which brings them in contact with worlds far removed from those of literary and artistic circles. One cannot generalize about how a poet should earn his living in this or in any conceivable society. But the worst thing for him, perhaps, from every point of view, would be to do nothing and care about nothing, except writing poetry.

So far, we have seen that earning a living and cultivating one's latent powers are not altogether easy to reconcile, and I have cited the special case of the poet, who wants to write poetry as well as earn a living and cultivate his latent powers. We may now ask whether the process of equipment to play one's part as a citizen may present any possible impediment to either of the other aims of education. It all depends on the content which we give to the idea of citizenship, and the means which we take to equip people for it. I think that the idea of the 'good citizen' is a moral concept; if so, we should expect the good citizen to be simply the good man manifesting his goodness in the social context. But we can still, I think, speak of a man as a good citizen whom we may regard as in some respect or other not a good man. A man may be devoted to the interests of his country, his region, or his city; he may sacrifice pleasure, comfort, popularity, in the public interest; wear out his energies in toiling for the public good; and yet be in private life vicious and dishonourable. To what extent can we call such a man a good citizen? It is strange, to me, that this elementary question, that of the relation of good citizenship to goodness, of public to private virtue, has not received the attention of writers on education such as Dr. Joad. Possibly the cultivation of virtue is regarded generally as the responsibility—the only responsibility—which educators leave to the parents. But the question of how far a bad man can be a good citizen is an interesting one in itself, and one about which Socrates, if he were alive today, would not fail to have something to say. For Dr. Joad, at least, it is clear that the ethical problem is one to be passed over, and that for him education in citizenship is education in applying intelligence to public affairs.

This becomes clear when he tells us of what Education in Citizenship should consist. First, those things which seem to him obvious. A child should be taught history, constitutional history (including instruction in how he is governed and how his governors are elected, and the structure of local as well as national government); biology and physiology, so that he may be made free (that is Dr. Joad's phrase) of the main facts, including the sexual facts, relating to the working of his own body; geography, and international affairs. This is a formidable programme for any child; and it is entirely training of the mind. I dare say that a knowledge of the main facts relating to the working of his own body might induce a child to brush his teeth morning and evening, if he were so rational a child as Dr. Joad must have been: most of us learn the habit first, and the reason for it later. There are perhaps a good many other things that the child could learn, merely in order to be a good citizen: jujitsu, to cope with burglars and footpads; first aid, in order to save the victims (for the Good Samaritan, from what little we know about him, seems to have had the makings of a good citizen). But my main comment on Dr. Joad's list of accomplishments is not that it is all simply book-learning, but that it omits any mention of training in moral behaviour and feeling. One would think that the good citizen was simply the well-informed citizen; but I am not convinced that a child, who, in Dr. Joad's words, 'carries at the back of his mind a political map of the modern world', will be better qualified to distinguish between good government and bad. Dr. Joad not only ignores what is generally called 'private' in favour of 'public' morality—thus ignoring the question whether we can ultimately draw any distinction between private and public morality; even his public morality appears to be merely a matter of being well-informed, and being trained to reason correctly.

Some of you may already have thought that I am devoting too much attention to Dr. Joad, who wrote a popular and very readable book called *About Education*. You may even have suspected that I have done this because his is the only book on the subject that I have read. You would somewhat exaggerate my illiteracy if you thought this: I have chosen Dr. Joad, partly because he puts a typical point of view so well—the point of view of the middle-brow intellectual who was reared on G. B. Shaw and H. G. Wells—for Dr. Joad is not very much younger than myself—and partly because his attitude towards education is implicit in statements sometimes made by more qualified educators. In a list of the aims of education by an authority whose name carries very much more weight in these matters than Dr. Joad's, I read that 'every man has a function as a man'. With this I do not disagree: every safety razor has a function as a safety razor. I then read, 'every man has a function as a citizen or subject of the society in which he lives.' With man's function as a man I shall try to cope later. Meanwhile, I may say that I do not see how his function as a citizen can be separated from his function as a man. I think the latter is the more important, but for reasons which I must postpone giving. But I return to my previous question, whether the really good citizen must not be also a good man; with the qualification that in certain contexts we are entitled to say that so-and-so is a 'good citizen', without committing ourselves to the assertion that he is a 'good man'. When it comes to training a young person, or, as Dr. Joad says, a child, to be a good citizen, I still think that it is important first to train him to become a good man.

There are incidental questions which we may ask. Democracy is the best form of society: on that we are all agreed. The chief point on which we do not agree is, as I have said before, what is a democracy. Most of us agree that democracy is of the parliamentary sort: that is, there are two parties, one in, one out, and neither party should be too long in or out. The government of our nation is, of course, rather more democratic when the party which we support is in, than when the other party is. I have been told that 'the function of the citizen of a democracy is to rule in turn for the good life of the whole'. Certainly, both parties, whether we call them Republican and Democrat, or Conservative and Labour, rule, when in office, for the good life of the whole: though none of them, when out of office, is likely to admit that the nation is being ruled for the good life of the whole. Certainly, in a democracy, every man should know how to rule and be ruled. To be wholly ruler, to be wholly ruled, is to lose humanity: and, in fact, the humblest worker needs to keep his own offspring in order, while the most powerful despot may be dominated, if by no constitutional powers, by wife, or mistress, or friends. The essential of a democracy is that there is no *total* rule: for total rule means that somebody is in control of affairs about some of which he is totally incompetent. In a democracy, scientists and scholars and artists should rule in their own spheres: it is not a democracy when a symphony can be deviationist, or a melancholy poem about an unhappy love affair defeatist and decadent, or a biological theory subversive.

It seems to me that we may raise the question, how far good citizenship can be an aim of a curriculum of education. To a large extent, surely, it must be the product of a training which is not consciously aimed at anything so comprehensive, and at the same time so narrowly defined as citizenship. The habits of accepting authority, of being able to exercise responsible freedom, of being able to exercise authority when compelled to assume it, are acquired unconsciously in early years. If parents are public-spirited people whose interests are not selfishly limited to themselves and their family, children will learn from their example (for the unconscious influence of parents is much more influential than their precepts) that they have a duty towards their neighbours, involving the assumption of responsibility and the exercise of self-control. And in so far as their mental capacities permit, they will learn that this duty involves not merely habitual responses, but thinking and making deliberate choices. In a school, they will learn adaptation to a larger community; and in a college, develop their public sense further in societies and voluntary activities.

Now when it is said that 'in a democracy the good man and the good citizen are identical', I do not disagree, but I should prefer to put it more generally and say simply, 'the good man and the good citizen are identical'. For the former proposition seems to imply another to this effect: 'in a state of society which is not a democracy one cannot be both a good man and a good citizen'. Now, under an evil system of government, the good man may sometimes realize his good citizenship by opposing that government. He will not, from the point of view of his rulers, be a good citizen; but then, from their point of view, he will not be a good man either. If good citizenship implies goodness, then there is something universal about good citizenship. Of course, we can say that the Christians martyred in the Roman persecutions were bad citizens; and from the point of view of their persecutors no doubt they were. Perhaps we may say, however, that in a democracy the good man has the greatest opportunity to exercise his goodness in citizenship; and the bad man the greatest opportunity to exercise his badness—or perhaps rather that in a democracy a greater number of good men, and a greater number of bad men, have this opportunity. This gives us a kind of definition of democracy, as the kind of society which offers these opportunities;

but observe also that while we arrive at our definition of democracy by the aid of the term 'citizenship', we are also implying a definition of good citizenship in terms of democracy.

I am afraid that when we pass from the term 'good man' to the term 'good citizen' we are insensibly passing from one shade of meaning of 'good' to another. But the test of the degree of difference is not found within the proposition itself, but in the further conclusions we draw: the difference may not appear until we have gone quite a long way. Similarly in the sentence 'since in a democracy all men are rulers, all men must have the education that rulers must have'. Now we see what this means, and we do not disagree; but I think that there are here two different shades of meaning of the word 'rulers'. An eminent British civil servant, a couple of years ago, gave a broadcast talk to explain UNESCO to his fellow-citizens, and said that UNESCO was a 'world club'. Now, one sees what he meant to convey; yet I could not help making the comment that a club was by definition an organization of which some people were not members: if everybody in the world were a member, it would cease to be a club. The difficulty here is not so extreme. But even though we agree that all men are rulers, we must not overlook differences in kind and degree of rule. If we think of any particular type of rulers, we can see that some of them need an education differing from that of other men: a judge of the Supreme Court is one kind of ruler, the conductor of an orchestra is another; and they have both had very specialized training, as well as special native aptitudes, to qualify them for the exercise of rule.

The difficulty, and the source of danger, is the application of the general statement about the aims of education, with which everyone can agree, to more concrete problems. From the general statement about education for citizenship we may pass, through the narrowing of the meaning to *political* activity, and through the narrowing of the meaning of education to what can be taught in classes and from books, to the putting of courses in citizenship into our curricula. I do not say that this is altogether a bad thing, though much could be transmitted by the intelligent teaching of history. It may even be necessary; but when it is, we should try to be quite clear as to why it is. It may be necessary as a palliative of conditions beyond the scope or control of the educational system. In so far as it is an attempt to educate the social conscience, to inculcate virtues, it is trying to supply a training which should be given by the family and the social environment, and is needed because the family and the social environment are not what they should be. In so far as it is the imparting of necessary or desirable knowledge and information, it may imply that the conduct of our society has become so complicated, the problems so interrelated, that it is beginning to make claims on the ordinary citizen greater than he can bear. For example, in earlier times foreign policy was the concern of only a very few persons in any nation; and it was only in relations with one foreign nation at a time—and with many foreign countries not at all—that the issues were so grave that it behooved every educated citizen to inform himself. Now we are all constantly concerned with what happens everywhere. The Spanish-American War was, it seemed at the time, nobody's business but that of the United States and Spain: nowadays, a war anywhere, even if of apparently small dimensions, is a matter of concern to everybody everywhere. I do not wish to pursue this minor question, but only to point the issue. By 'education for citizenship' we may mean training in the essential faculties which are necessary both in the conduct of one's personal affairs and in forming an opinion about public policy: the ability to reason, to weigh evidence, to decide how much one needs to know in order to make up one's mind, and the ability to perceive the fundamental moral differences of right and wrong and apply them. And, so far as these things can be taught, they can be inculcated through the study of history. But we may also mean courses of study in all the manifold social problems of contemporary life: in political theory, in public finance, in economics, in municipal government, or in the whole field now covered by sociology, several very vital questions arise. At what age should these studies be begun? And how much time should be given to them at each stage? I do not believe that you can teach these things, beyond a point, to those who are not going to be individually concerned with them; because most of us cannot study very deeply any subject which does not concern us as individuals, which concerns us only as *members*. I do not mean that nobody should be deeply concerned with these matters: that would be absurd. But those who are deeply concerned with them, and justifiably concentrate their attention on them, are those who are going to make their living thereby, and what is more important, to express themselves by making active contributions. That is, the subjects to which we can profitably give the most attention are those in which we hope to excel. The desire to vote always for the right candidate cannot become the ambition of a lifetime.

Education for citizenship, then, seems to mean first of all the developing of social conscience; and I have already suggested that 'social' conscience can only be a development of 'conscience': the moment we talk about 'social conscience' and forget conscience, we are in moral danger—just as 'social justice' must be based upon 'justice'. The separation in our minds which results simply from dwelling constantly upon the adjective 'social' may lead to crimes as well as errors. In the name of social justice we can excuse, or justify to ourselves, or simply ignore, injustice: in the name of social conscience we can do the same by conscience. The same sort of substitutions can occur with the word 'democracy'. 'Social democracy' sounds at first a phrase to which no one could object; but the denotation can be so manipulated that it can be made to point to something which to most of us, I think, may be anything but 'democratic'.

What I hope has emerged from this wild-goose chase is that our list of three aims of education—the professional, the social and the development of all of the latent powers and faculties—is one in which each aim is implicated with the others, and also that each one may be pursued in such a way as to interfere with the others. This is due to the applications we make of each of three undisputed propositions; and to the fact that in each step of the inferences we make, we may be applying narrower and questionable definitions of a word which in the original proposition did not need to be defined. I have so far said least about the incorrect inferences we may draw from 'the development of the latent powers and faculties' or, if we are not merely thinking of hobbies and recreations, what Arnold called the 'pursuit of perfection'. I once knew a man who, being of independent means, planned a comprehensive humanistic education for himself. I am not quite sure to what studies he applied himself at an American university, but they did not include Latin and Greek, because he deferred these until he should get to Oxford or Cambridge, where he thought he would have them at their best; or modern languages and literatures, because he intended, after Oxford or Cambridge, to spend a year or two at universities in France, Germany, and Italy in turn. An extensive course of travel was to crown this culture. Needless to say he never completed the programme. The pursuit of perfection, or of comprehensive culture, is not enough, because it is a by-product of our desire to *do* something. To perfect oneself, so far as one can, and in the ways in which one is perfectible, may be a duty, but only in relation to some aim beyond oneself. To this point I shall return later.

I propose to turn now to the question of the general presuppositions, assumptions, or conscious social and political theories upon which any theory of education must be based. In closing, however, I should like to quote a contemporary French writer, Gustave Thibon; from his introduction to that very profound and original book *La Pesanteur et la grâce* by Simone Weil. It is the thought of Simone Weil which he is expounding:

'The soul devoted to the pursuit of the absolutely good meets in this world with insoluble contradictions. "Our life is impossibility, absurdity. Everything that we will is contradicted by the conditions or by the consequences attached to it. That is because we are ourselves contradiction, being merely creatures . . ." If, for example, you have innumerable children: that tends to bring about overpopulation and war (the typical case is Japan). If you improve the material conditions of the people: you risk spiritual deterioration. If you devote yourself utterly to some person—you cease to exist for that person. Only imaginary goods imply no contradiction: the girl who desires a large family, the social reformer who dreams of the happiness of the people—such individuals do not encounter any obstacle so long as they refrain from action. They sail along happily in a good which is absolute, but fictitious: to stumble against reality is the signal for waking up. This contradiction, the mark of our wretchedness and our greatness, is something that we must accept in all its bitterness.'[1]

[1] 'L'âme attachée à la poursuite du bien pur se heurte ici-bas a d'irréductibles contradictions. "Notre vie est impossibilité, absurdité. Chaque chose que nous voulons est contradictoire avec les conditions ou les conséquences qui y sont attachées. C'est que nous sommes nous-mêmes contradiction, étant des créatures . . ." Ayez par exemple des enfants sans compter: vous favorisez la surpopulation et la guerre (le cas du Japon est typique à cet égard); améliorez le sort matériel du peuple: vous risquez d'altérer son âme: dévouez-vous entièrement à quelqu'un: vous cessez d'exister pour lui, etc. Seul le bien imaginaire ne comporte pas de contradiction: la jeune fille qui désire une nombreuse posterité, le réformateur social qui rêve le bonheur du peuple, etc. ne se heurtent à aucun obstacle tant qu'ils ne passent pas à l'action: ils voguent à pleine voile dans un bien pur, mais fictif; le choc contre le réel est le signal du reveil. Cette contradiction, signe de notre misère et de notre grandeur, nous devons l'accepter dans toute son amertume.' Thibon, quoting Weil, in his preface to *La Pesanteur et la grace* (Paris, Plon, 1950, pp. XX–XXI).

THE AIMS OF EDUCATION

3. The Conflict between Aims

We have already observed that the term 'education' has become more difficult of definition as a result of social changes in the last three or four hundred years. We may distinguish four important phases. In the first, we were concerned only with the training of a small minority for certain learned professions. In the second, with the refinement of culture, we were concerned with the education of the gentleman, or of the *honnête homme*; and at the same time, with the supply of the rudiments of literacy to a humbler stratum of society. During the nineteenth century, the minds of educators were largely occupied with the problem of extending the benefits, or supposed benefits, of education as then understood, to an increasing number of the population. The problem was apparently simple: men still thought that they knew what education was—it was what a part of the community had been receiving; and so long as this education could be supplied to increasing numbers, educators felt that they were on the right road. But today we realize that we have come near enough to the end of expansion to be faced with a wholly new problem. It is parallel to the end of geographical expansion. In the nineteenth century, the United States was still pushing westward; European nations were still staking claims for themselves in colonial empire.

Now the area of geographical expansion is over—at least, by the methods employed in the previous century. In the nineteenth century, there seemed also to be only the problem of educating more of the members of society. But now we are at a stage at which we are not simply trying to educate more people—we are already committed to providing everybody with something called education. We are coming to the end of our educational frontier. Long ago we decided that everybody must be taught to read, write and cipher; and so long as there were large numbers who could not read, write, or cipher, we did not need to look too closely into the question of what education meant. Every stage of development of our society presents us not only with new, but with more difficult problems, as well as with the same problems in more difficult forms: for we have now to cope with a new illiteracy, and a much more difficult illiteracy to overcome—namely, the illiteracy of that part of the population which has had its elementary schooling but has become illiterate through lack of occasion to use what it has been taught. This secondary illiteracy is a new phenomenon. It is aggravated by the effects of radio and cinema, and by the replacement, in popular periodicals, of words by pictures. I am convinced that readers in England—readers of *anything*—can be classified partly according to the size of type to which they can give attention. One can say that the educated man is one who can read the reports of Parliamentary debates, and the reports of important law cases, from beginning to end—skipping intelligently, of course. There is a large number who can read a few paragraphs, if the type is large enough. There is an increasing proportion of the population which can read only headlines of any part of a newspaper not concerned with sport or crime.

This is a kind of parenthesis, illustrative of the fact that even illiteracy—even analphabetism—is not a problem that can be finished with and written off. My point is that now that we are committed to giving everybody formal instruction, everything must be called into question and examined—the forms, the subject matter, the methods, the purposes. So we have always new problems, and the old ones in new forms.

What happens in our thinking about education is, of course, only a special instance of what is happening to human consciousness. In the world today we find ourselves more and more trying consciously to manipulate what had been left to take its own course—that is, our area of conscious manipulation becomes bigger and bigger. A problem comes into existence through our ability to become aware of it; the awareness shapes the problem; and once we are conscious of a problem, we cannot dismiss it from consciousness; we find ourselves under obligation to try to find an answer.

By an 'educational system'—whether we are considering a particular institution, or the general organization of instruction in which we can distinguish national characteristics—we mean something which is a compound of *growth* and *construction*. I accept the view which refers to 'the relativity of educational theory and practice to a prevailing order,' and I agree with Professor Adolf Lowe when he says:

'. . . no system of education can be truly appreciated or criticized except against the background of the social order in which it operates. The reason for this is that education always serves a social purpose, even if both teacher and pupil are unaware of the fact and experience the educational contact as an entirely spontaneous undertaking. Actually at each stage, from elementary to university education, powerful social forces are at work, moulding the maturing individual according to a pattern, thus aiming at creating a definite human type.'[1]

I have only two comments to make on this quotation: first, that the 'powerful social forces' may be *more* or *less* conscious; and may consist of the influence of a dominant class, or of a prevailing attitude towards life of the society as a whole, or they may be concentrated, in a totalitarian regime, in the deliberate aims of the leaders of a political party. Second, we must recognize that the system of education in every country is the product of history, and reflects the history, and responds to the temperament, of that people. In so far as a system of education is something shaped by the conscious aims of a few men—whether these men are organizing the education of their own people, or creating a system for some more backward race—there is always grave danger of borrowing or imposing something which does not fit the ethos, the way of life, the habits of thought and feeling of that people. In America we have seen different aims and methods promoted by educators biased by an enthusiasm for German, or French, or English systems of education, respectively—educators who were

[1] Lowe, *The Universities in Transformation* (Christian News Letter Books No. 9, London, Macmillan).

sometimes themselves partly educated in one or other of these countries. The intellectual formation of a man like President Eliot of Harvard, himself partly the product of the German system, led, I think, to an exaggerated application of German methods. On the other hand, I think it is very likely that the model of English institutions in India, and of Western educational methods in the East in general, was too hurriedly and confidently imposed. But the confusion of the imitation of various European systems in America, and of Western–including American–methods in the East, is now in danger of becoming more general, as every part of the world becomes more aware of every other; as the concentration of wealth and power shifts from one nation to another; and as a greater uniformity of culture seems likely to result from the pressure of one civilization upon another.

In the changes of which I have been speaking, in the continual enlargement of the area of human planning, it is apparent that we are living in an age in which *construction* has priority over *growth*. This is a development which we must accept. We have not time to wait, or to leave things to be fought out between various natural forces. We live in an age when towns have to be designed, when we have to have regulations about the type of building, the height of building, and the uses to which building may be put, in every city area. And in such an age we also find ourselves obliged to be more conscious about what we are doing in our educational institutions. Only we must remember that being more conscious about everything is a very great strain, for it imposes a greater and greater responsibility upon fewer and fewer people. The psychological and physiological strain upon the member of a government cabinet today, the strain of being head of a government, or even secretary of state or foreign minister, is almost greater than any human being should be asked to bear.

We must be prepared then, so far ahead as we can descry anything, for a tendency to universal standardization in education everywhere. When, a couple of years ago, it was announced that an agreement had been reached for standardization of nuts and bolts between Britain and the United States, so that we should be able to buy a nut in one country and fit it to a screw in the other, the announcement appeared in very small print, but it struck me as the most important news of the day. It was also a portent. And the other thing for which we must be prepared is greater and greater intervention and control of education by the State. And when I say 'the State,' I do not mean Illinois or any other state–I mean the central government in every country. It has been formally a fact in certain European countries; but in all countries I think that the State is likely to find itself more obliged to pay the piper, and therefore more impelled to call the tune.

There are obvious material reasons for this. Educational institutions, especially the big universities, become more and more expensive to run. They become bigger, they need always more buildings, more staff, and their maintenance involves a higher and higher proportion of administrative and financial work. They need bigger and bigger libraries and museums; more and better laboratories; and scientific equipment becomes more and more elaborate and costly. At the same time, the endowments bring diminishing returns, and the private sources from which new endowments flowed are running dry. In the end, perhaps bankruptcy might lead to the universities' having to be taken over by the State or closed down. But on the other hand, the central governments become more and more interested in what the universities do. (I am, I ought to say, thinking of conditions in Britain: how far these observations apply to conditions in America is for you to judge. The British government, owing to the great expansion of the Civil Service, is a very large employer of labour: the requirements of the Civil Service become more varied and specialized, and must be satisfied by recruits from all the universities.) Also, every government today is more and more concerned with the advances of science in such ways as the governments find needful. If the universities are not equipped to pursue the kind of research, and provide men trained in the specialities that the governments require, then the universities must be provided with the funds–and directed in the use of them.

Nobody dislikes totalitarian government more than I do; but

it is not enough merely to hate it, or to concentrate our detestation upon its uglier manifestations elsewhere. We must at least recognize the existence of pressures which are modifying society everywhere, if only in order to be alert to counteract them and to accept nothing that we can do without. Not all men are moved by unscrupulous love of power, or by fanatical ideology: men sometimes find themselves in a position where they have to assume more power than they want—or in a position in which the assumption of power may plausibly seem to be the only way of meeting some crisis or relieving some intolerable situation. And if it comes to seem more and more important for the centralized State to control every branch of instruction, to exercise the ultimate control, then the 'social purpose' of education will come to be identified with the 'social purpose' of the head of the department of State responsible for education.

I have been following a rather tortuous course to lead to a question which really started me on it. In what I wrote about education several years ago, a critic finds an inconsistency. He says, 'Mr. Eliot's chief complaint of other writers on education is that they seek to use the schools to achieve social purposes they have at heart. Then he falls into the pit he has digged for others: he wants to use the schools to advance social purposes of his own.' Now, I do not think that anybody can think seriously about education who is devoid of social purposes of his own; and I am sure that these social purposes will guide him towards some of his conclusions about education. For anyone who denies that education should have a social purpose will be omitting something without which it is not education. But I think that anyone who considers education in relation to social purpose should try to be quite clear as to what social purposes guide his own theory of education; which are peculiar to himself, or to a group whose views are not shared by some other group; which he believes to apply to the society to which he and his sympathizers belong; and which, if any, apply to every society.

What I have been saying before, therefore, was intended to elicit the fact that the meaning of the term 'social purpose' is subject to a good deal of variation. In a liberal democracy it should mean something discernible in the mind and temperament of the people as a whole, something arising out of its common ethos, which finds expression through a variety of intellectual leaders holding varied and sometimes conflicting opinions. In a totalitarian society, it may mean something formulated in the brains of a few persons in power, deduced from a particular political-social theory, and imposed by every means of compulsion and indoctrination, so that it may in time become integrated into the common ethos. This is a very different kind of social purpose. In a liberal society every writer on the subject will have some social purpose of his own; something he wishes to retain, restore, or introduce through the means of education. Therefore he should know himself how far his assumptions are his own, and how far he is justified in assuming that they are shared by all intelligent men of good will. He should, in short, examine his premises.

Now as education, it has been agreed, has several aims, the social purposes have to be guarded from interfering with the other aims; and also, we have to allow for the possibility that we may have several social purposes which have to be reconciled to each other. I remind you of the sage words of Gustave Thibon and Simone Weil, which I have already quoted. I shall take as an illustration 'the ideal of equality of opportunity,' because my previous reservations on the applicability of that ideal seem to have provoked especially strong dissent. This ideal certainly expresses a social purpose, and is equally applicable to other things than education: education is merely one of the benefits to which men and women should ideally have equal opportunity. This ideal has two very strong grounds of appeal, which must be distinguished. One is that ability is wasted, of which society has need, through our failing to recognize and train it. This is a utilitarian argument; it has force, but of a very different kind from the second. This is, that it is not just that any person should be prevented, by our failure to educate him, from the full development of his latent powers and faculties. The second seems to me the more universal and compelling, because it is a *moral* ground. Now on this ground at least, the assertion that every child should have equal opportunity for education is one which nobody will deny. The only difficulty comes when we proceed, from cherishing this ideal, to attempt to realize it; and when we give it priority, in our educational schemes, over other ideals of education.

If we pursued the ideal of equality of opportunity rigorously we should, it seems to me, have to see to it that no educational institution was superior to any other professing to supply the same grade of education. We should certainly have to see to it that no institution gave a better education simply because it could charge higher fees, and select its pupils for any other reason than intellectual promise. To what extent do the pupils at expensive private schools get a better education? What is it that their parents are paying for? I know that the motives from which affluent parents choose a school are often motives which have nothing to do with education. There is the desire that their children should mix with other children of the same economic status and social type; there is also the calculation that their children will make the sort of friends who will be 'useful' to them in later life; there is also the simple snobbism attached to the name of a particular school or university. But there are better reasons than these: there is the attraction of a foundation with traditions, and a long list of distinguished alumni. And there is the best reason of all, especially for the private school—for it is in school days that this reason is the most cogent: the parents know that their child will be a member of a small group, that he will be taught in a class of fifteen or twenty instead of in a class of forty or fifty. Anyone who has ever tried to teach young children knows that the larger your class is, beyond fifteen or twenty, the less you can teach.

It is certainly desirable that every school in the country should have enough accommodation, and enough teachers, to be able to teach children in smaller groups. I thought, in 1944, that the Education Act of that year—an attempt, certainly, to improve state education—put the wrong things first. Instead of extending immediately the years of compulsory education, and thus adding to the number of pupils, we should in my opinion have aimed first at the supply of more teachers and accommodation for those already in the state-supported or -aided schools; and undertaken to give better teaching than we do, to those under fourteen. But when will we, in any country, provide the money for this reform? Again, before we train more teachers, we ought to consider whether we are paying our present teachers adequately. I have never worked in a coal mine, or a uranium mine, or in a herring trawler; but I know from experience that working in a bank from 9:15 to 5:30, and once in four weeks the whole of Saturday, with two weeks' holiday a year, was a rest cure compared to teaching in a school.

I am told that 'no American advocate of equality of opportunity would argue that the rich should be forbidden to set up schools of their own, which might turn out to be superior to those supported by the State.' This is advocacy of a limited equality, an equality qualified by a good deal of inequality. If the schools established by the rich for the rich turn out to be better schools (though I do not believe this is altogether true) then what becomes of equality of opportunity? And how can we limit our equality to an equal opportunity to get a good education? If one child has better opportunities in life than another, merely because his parents are richer, will not many people regard this situation as unjust? It would seem that inequality in education is merely a special instance of inequality in general, and if we affirm a principle in one area are we not driven to accept it in all? Certainly, some English advocates of equality in education would go much further than, as I am told, American advocates do: they would abolish the private school and the privately endowed institution, or bring them all into the state system.

The usefulness of the phrase 'equality of opportunity' is confused by the various meanings which we attach to the word 'opportunity'–it means different things to different people, and different things to the same people at different moments, often without our knowing it. That everyone should, as far as we can make it possible, be able to pursue the activity for which he is best fitted, is an aim which we can all applaud. One has sometimes observed the son of people in well-to-do circumstances, admirably qualified by talent and temperament to be a first-rate garage mechanic, yet never having the opportunity to become one. Pressure of family and environment, the acquirement of tastes incompatible with the occupation for which he is best fitted, and perhaps also a defective education, usually stand in his way. I am afraid that to most people at most times 'opportunity' means a good many other things than the opportunity to develop the latent powers and capacities: it means opportunity to make money, to acquire a higher social status, to have power over others. For some young women, opportunity means opportunity to get a screen test; and only a small number of those who crave this opportunity deserve it. In short, opportunity is an empty term unless we can answer the question 'opportunity for what?'

It would seem, then, that most of the time, when we talk of 'equality of opportunity,' we either do not know what we mean, or do not mean what we say, or else are driven to conclusions from which most people would shrink. It is avoiding the issue if we assume vaguely that 'inequality' means only the injustice of overprivileged and underprivileged social classes. It may happen that a child at a state school finds a teacher who will elicit his aptitude for a particular subject, and that a child at an expensive private school has just the wrong teacher. But what about overprivileged and underprivileged areas in the same country? A poor state or country may not be able to provide such good equipment or teachers, such good libraries or laboratories, as a richer one. Should not that inequality be redressed also? Thus the claim of equality of opportunity, if pressed to its logical conclusion, seems to me to lead inescapably to a universal and exclusive state system of education, to the cost of which the richer parts of the country, like the richer individuals, will contribute proportionately, but from which they will derive only the same educational returns as their poorer neighbours. And next, is it just that the citizens of a wealthy or advanced nation should have greater opportunity for education than those of a backward one? Unless we maintain that some races or peoples are superior to others we seem to be forced toward the goal of a world system of education. And finally, if we are to have complete equality of opportunity in education, it seems to follow that we must have a uniform system for grading the intelligence of pupils, so that each shall receive just the kind and amount of education to which his gifts entitle him.

If, as I have suggested, the thoroughgoing application of the principle of equality of opportunity (reinforced by the other pressures of which I have spoken) tends towards increased control by the State, then the State will have something to say about opportunity. It will find itself limiting opportunity to those vocations which serve the ends of the State as conceived by those who happen to control the State. I am not suggesting that it would, in a Western democracy, reach the point of direction of labour; but by offering greater inducements and advantages and facilities in one direction rather than another, it might tend to limit education to the kinds of training which served the immediate purposes of the State.

The idea of equal opportunity, it would seem, has to be considered in relation to each of the three aims of education from which we started; and it might be that in this connection, also, one aim would be pursued in such a way as to interfere with another. The difficulty arises from the fact that we cannot, in practice, wholly separate one from another. There have been, no doubt, men who were animated by curiosity and the thirst for knowledge, to such a degree as to be able to pursue their studies quite apart from their actual calling in life. There have been Spinozas who, in order to be free to exercise a wholly unremunerative activity and one not regarded by the world as particularly useful, have been content to earn a modest livelihood by grinding lenses. There have been other men, in humble positions, in whom the speculative or contemplative motive has been so strong that they found happiness in this double life. On the other hand, there have been men so completely limited in interest to the duties of their occupation that they have seemed to be hardly more than machines. Most men escape from this only by way of recreations and hobbies, ordinarily of a rather trivial nature. The ideal is a life in which one's livelihood, one's function as a citizen, and one's self-development all fit into and enhance each other. For most of us, the full pursuit of any of these aims must interfere with another;

and we are obliged, at best, to make almost day-to-day calculations and decisions between the several claims. We are all limited, by circumstances if not by capacities. To get anything you want you find you have to sacrifice something else that you want; and in getting it, you find that you have to accept other things that you do not want. Yet we must maintain that a man is not educated if he is merely trained to a trade or profession; that he has to play his part as a citizen; and that, as a citizen, to be something more than a voting machine, and, as a worker, to be something more than a working machine, he must be trained and developed to something more than citizenship and work. And we find that the principle of 'equal opportunity' is meaningless—that is, susceptible of being interpreted by everybody in terms of what he *desires*, instead of what he ought to desire—unless we answer the question 'opportunity for what?'

There are obviously some 'opportunities' which ought to be available to everyone. Every man should have the opportunity of earning a livelihood in reasonable and decent conditions; of marrying and rearing a family who will also have the same opportunity; of rest and recreation, and so forth. You will observe that this sentence is made up of terms which will have different meanings in different social contexts: it is necessarily vague. But when we proceed beyond material necessities we get into a region of values. And so the assertion of 'equal opportunity' leads us gradually to the point at which we must know what we mean by 'the good life'. The question 'What is education?' or the question 'What is the aim of education?' leads us to this point. Now it is unlikely that we shall all agree on an answer to the final question, 'What is Man?' Therefore, what we mean in practice by 'education' will be the highest common factor of what enough educated people mean by it. So you may say that 'education' is likely to mean, in practice, a compromise between what different people mean by it.

I hope that it is by now clear that I do not complain of other writers that 'they seek to use the schools to achieve social purposes which they have at heart.' When we talk about education, we cannot stop at education as if it were a field which we could close off; an area in which we could come to agreement whatever our differences of philosophy. We must have a social purpose in education, and therefore, if we talk about education, we must be prepared to make clear to ourselves and to our hearers what our social purpose is. But the social purpose itself should not spring from a prejudice, an emotional bias in favour of equality or hierarchy, a bias in favour of freedom or of order. Nor is the social purpose in itself enough, for it does not take account of the whole nature of man.

We have seen that, just as we are led, the moment we begin to think seriously about education, to think about citizenship, so thinking about citizenship leads us to something beyond citizenship; for the good citizen in the end turns out to be the good man; and that leads wherever the whole problem of ethics is going to take us. Now a view of education such as Dr. Joad's, which suggests that training for citizenship and training for the development of one's latent powers and faculties can be carried on in separate departments, may seem clear enough about the discipline for citizenship, but offers no general prescription for the development, or we may say 'the improvement' of man as man. As citizens, men must hold certain principles in common, and must agree on certain social habits; the fact of having to get on with other people imposes some discipline. But in the question of the development of latent powers, this view does not proceed to maintain that there are certain latent powers for good, and certain latent powers for evil, in man as man; it suggests rather, that each man has latent powers and faculties peculiar to himself, illustrated by the various ways in which men spend their leisure time. It is perfectly true that some men have an aptitude for and take enjoyment in doing their own repairs about the house; whereas others are much better advised to send for a plumber, a carpenter, or an electrician. I have no doubt that when Dr. Joad talks of latent powers and faculties, he is thinking of higher powers and faculties than those of the handy man. Nevertheless, he is leaving the area of latent powers and faculties uncontrolled. The danger of separation between the social and the private life—which has the corollary that the only criterion of morals is whether one's conduct is harmful to one's neighbours, and that every man should be free to do as he likes with *himself*–is that the social code, the code of citizenship, will become more and more constrictive, more and more exercising a pressure towards *conformity*; and that this public servitude to society will be compensated by extreme licence in whatever conduct is supposed to be none of society's business.

It is true that in a society organized on this principle the social may prove in the end to encroach more and more upon the private. In a society organized to carry out this principle, the rules of matrimony and sexual relations may be, at first, much relaxed. But then it may be found that this relaxation has undesirable social consequences–that it affects the birth rate unfavourably, in a nation which finds that it needs more workmen and soldiers; or that it has an unfortunate effect upon the children, who may begin to show psychological aberrations, or may grow up to be less desirable citizens than the government wants them to be: and then private life will be interfered with in the name of society. People may be ordered to have larger families, or to have no families at all, according to whether they are judged to be suitable breeders of future citizens. Thus the individual may find his privacy, his opportunity for exercising his moral freedom and responsibility gradually taken away from him in the name of society.

The restoration of a kind of order in people's private lives, however, when it is made in the name of a social purpose only, furthers the reduction of men to machines, and is the opposite from the development of their humanity. The assumption that you can have areas of control, and areas of complete freedom, must lead either to a suffocating uniformity of order, or to chaos. The actual degree of freedom or control may differ between one area and another. We are all more willing to submit to regulation of our public than of our private behaviour, and gradually, with the increasing complexity of modern civilization, we are prepared to submit to more and more regulations in the public interest. There are still people who object to being vaccinated, but few people now resent being isolated when they have typhoid fever. Most people recognize that the state of their drains is a matter in which they have a duty to their neighbours; though not everybody recognizes that he has the same duty in respect to the noise of his radio set. In a flat, one expects to have less freedom in many petty details of life than in a solitary cottage in the country. On the other hand, people in England since the war have objected, and they have my sympathy, to being forbidden to set up a tool shed in a country garden without a licence from the government, or being forced to employ a workman to do what they are capable of doing themselves. Fortunately, we do not yet submit to universal regulation in the public interest; and fortunately, we are still capable of being shocked by private behaviour, even when it does not appear to injure anyone but the culprit himself. And so long as we are capable of resenting control, and of being shocked by other people's private lives, we are still human. We are, at least, recognizing that man is something more than merely a social animal: that there should be limitations to social control. And by being shocked (when it is something more than a prejudice that is shocked) we are recognizing, however dimly, that there is some law of behaviour which is something more than a duty to the State.

What, then, should we mean by the development of the individual's latent powers and faculties, if we go further than Dr. Joad, and consider the individual, not as if he were a seed out of a packet with no name on it, which we plant and tend out of curiosity to see what it will become, and what sort of flower or fruit it will bear; but as a seed of a known plant which has been cultivated for many generations—a plant about which we know what its flower or fruit ought to be, if it receives the right nurture and grows to perfection? How are we to try to educate good men, seeing that the idea of the good citizen implies the good man? Are we to be content with a rough-and-ready description of the good citizen, leaving everybody to define goodness according to his own taste and fancy? As you may have feared, this question raises for me the final question, that of the relation of education to religion.

THE AIMS OF EDUCATION

4. The Issue of Religion

We have, so far, arrived (I hope) at the conclusion that there is a reciprocal implication between education for citizenship, or as a social being, and the development of the latent powers of the individual, or the improvement of 'man as man'. A man cannot be altogether a good citizen unless he is also a good man; and the wholly good man must also be a good citizen—at least in the sense that he is one who cares for the good of his neighbours. The distinction, and the relationship, are similar to that between work and play. There is something wrong when a man gets no enjoyment from his work; and to play any game properly you have to work at it.

Even, however, if we recognize the mutual implication of citizenship and individual development, we still lack a standard by which to measure one or the other. We therefore incline to take either as the standard for the other in different contexts. In one context, citizenship is undefined; we take for granted that whatever it means, we all understand it; and our notion of individual development will be adapted to the undefined citizenship. In another context, we may do exactly the reverse. The limitation to one point of view will tend to make us either authoritarians, placing strict limitations upon the exercise of individual choice or caprice; the limitation to the other point of view will make us libertarians, holding, as some people have, that the best government is that which governs the least. The latter will tend to believe that human beings are naturally good, and that left to themselves they will flower into good citizens; the former that you can make them good by enforcing good laws—or else, that the residue of a human being's behaviour, beyond what can be controlled by legislation, does not matter. And in this contest it is likely to be the authoritarians who will win, because authority is a short cut to dealing with abuses and injustices; and the contexts in which we are members of a mass are more compulsive than those in which we are individuals. In the latter, we stand alone; and it is easier to submit to an authority with which we identify ourselves than to tolerate nonconformity in others.

Although we may at this point agree that citizenship and individual development imply each other, we lack an outside standard by which citizenship and individual development can both be measured; for the measurement by each other leaves us in a vicious circle of illusory definition, defining each in turn in terms of the other. We have found that 'the improvement of man as man' is an empty phrase, unless we can agree about what is improvement; and that we cannot agree about this unless we find a common answer to the question 'What is Man?' Now we cannot expect to agree to one answer to this question; for with this question, our differences will turn out in the end to be religious differences; and it does not matter whether you are a 'religious person' or not, or whether you expressly repudiate everything that you call 'a religion'; there will be some sort of religious attitude—even if you call it a nonreligious attitude—implied in your answer.

There are two questions which have to be distinguished: that of the place of religion in education, and that of the place of education in religion. The first is the question with which we are more familiar. To the question of the place of religion in education, there are several answers. The most important seem to be the following:

1. Where the State itself professes allegiance to a particular religion, or religious denomination, this religion may be affirmed, and taught, in all the educational institutions controlled by the State; and the teaching will be in conformity with the doctrines of this religion. Private institutions, for those who profess another religion or branch of the same religion, and for those who object to all religious teaching, may under such a system be either tolerated or suppressed: but as the

suppression of every form of religious teaching except that of the official religion of the State seems to me unchristian, I am not concerned with this extreme. (All educational foundations might be religious, and none specially favoured by the State. As this would be an accidental situation, implying that the State itself should take no responsibility for education, it is a purely hypothetical situation which need not concern us.)

2. The complete separation of religious instruction from instruction in other subjects. This means that in schools and colleges no religious beliefs would be taken for granted or inculcated. Religious instruction would be reserved for the home, the Sunday school, and of course the theological training college.

3. The imparting in schools of such religious instruction as represents the common belief of the greatest part of the local society, leaving the doctrines of any particular denomination to be taught by the parents and their church. This is more or less the intention of the Education Act of 1944: it is, of course, qualified by concessions to those parents who wish their children excused from this religious instruction, either on the ground of wanting more specific doctrine or that of another religion, or of objecting to religious teaching of any kind.

4. A mixed system, in which no religion is taught in the State schools, but in which the adherents of any religion may set up denominational schools for their own children.

These are, I believe, the chief ways of dealing with the problem of religion in education. They are all, unfortunately, unsatisfactory.

We may group together the first and the second of these systems as being based on a principle, and the third and fourth as based on expediency. In drawing this distinction I am not making any value judgment: an inconsistent method may work better than a consistent one. I am merely saying that the expedient systems are not logically defensible. If the denominational school embodies the correct theory of the relation of religion to education, then it is deplorable that the greater part of the population should be deprived of its advantages; if the secular school embodies the correct theory, then it is questionable whether the denominational school should not be, to put it mildly, discouraged. (Of course, in practice, they are not so different as all that: education in secular schools does not necessarily quench religious faith in its products, and the pupils who have been educated in denominational schools frequently disencumber themselves of such religious education as they have received, very soon after they go out into the world.) Not only cannot both systems be right; the denominations cannot all be right either. Nor can the supporter of the schools of his church be altogether satisfied with his privileges. For he must be aware that his schools are tolerated by outsiders because they represent too small a minority to be worth suppressing, or because they represent too powerful a minority to suppress. He must be aware also that the costs of equipping a modern university are so great that his own church cannot supply itself with enough to go round, and that great numbers of young people will proceed from their church schools into a very different atmosphere: in England, certainly, there is no great university in which the religious foundation is now anything but vestigial.

The introduction into state-provided schools of such religious instruction as can be agreed upon as representing the common beliefs of the largest Christian sects is an experiment of the Education Act of 1944. This is a compromise between teaching the tenets of one particular denomination, and leaving religious education altogether to parents and Sunday schools. What its effect may be remains to be seen. Behind it, however, there is a remarkable theory of which its promoters were no doubt unaware. It is implicitly an assertion that 'Christianity' is simply what all Christians believe in common, and that this is what is essential; that the differences are unimportant; and that it is possible to be a satisfactory Christian without belonging to any church. In this way the State may be initiating a theological doctrine of its own, in contradiction to all the churches. Children are to be taught in schools all that is necessary to be a Christian; leaving to the parents the option of teaching them what is necessary to be Episcopalian, Methodist, Presbyterian, Congregationalist or Baptist—just as they may have private lessons in piano or violin. That is the theory. The *tendency* would be, if it went to the whole length of that unlikely course, for the several churches to be supplanted by a new State Christianity. For the implication of teaching only a part of Christianity is that that is the only part which matters.

So much for the third and fourth methods. I have said that the first and second are defensible in principle. The first, that in which all State schools will teach the tenets of a particular religion and communion, is possible only under one of two conditions. Either the nation must be homogeneous in religion, so that the official religion of the State is that of the vast majority of individual citizens, or else a dictatorial government must impose its own doctrines on the mass of society—or at least impose a conformity of outward profession—by discipline, inoculation, or fraud. For such despotism there is nothing to be said. The former is possible only in a few countries, and even in these it presents dangers so grave that it may become as unsatisfactory as any other. It may lead to the control of the Church by the State, or to the control of the State by the Church: two situations between which there may not be much to choose. But it has one striking advantage in theory at least. From my point of view, it does not matter in this particular context whether the Church established in education is a national Church with a national head, or an international Church with an international head. If a National Church, then it should have a hierarchy independent of the State, and prepared if necessary to oppose the State; but where the hierarchy is itself composed of clerics appointed by the State, we have to rely on the State not to appoint men who will be subservient to it. In either case, an authoritative and independent church is desirable for meeting the difficulty which I raised earlier in connection with the third of our 'aims of education'. I said that the second aim, 'training for citizenship', was directed by the meaning of citizenship represented by an outside authority, in relation to which the individual has defined rights, responsibilities, and duties of submission; and that the third aim, 'develop latent powers', or 'improve man as man', was left to every individual, or at least to every educator, to interpret as he pleases. It is the province of our religious teachers to instruct us in our latent powers and tell us which are good and which are bad, and to give a definite meaning to the improvement of 'man as man'. We need a Church capable of conflict with the State as well as of co-operation with it. We need a Church to protect us from the State, and to define the limits of our rights, responsibilities, and duties of submission in relation to our rights, and to our responsibilities and duties to ourselves and towards God. And, owing to human fallibility, we may sometimes need the State to protect us against the Church. Too close identification of the two can lead to oppression from which there is no escape.

The system in which instruction in schools and colleges is purely secular, leaving religious instruction to parents and voluntary Sunday schools, appears at first to be the antithesis of that which I have just been discussing. It achieves consistency by attempting to leave out the third aim of education, or at least by limiting the meaning of 'latent powers' to 'capacities for everything except spiritual life', and the meaning of 'the improvement of man as man' to 'the improvement of man as the highest of the apes, or as *homo faber et ludens*'—but not as a son of God. But the assertion that a man's religion is his private affair, that from the point of view of society it is irrelevant, may turn out in the end to lead to a situation very favourable to the establishment of a religion, or a substitute for religion, by the State. The religious sense, and the sense of community, cannot be finally divorced from each other. They are first formed, certainly, in the family; and when they are defective in the family, the defect cannot be supplied by the school and the university. But on the other hand, the contrast between a community life in which religion has no place, and a family life for which it is reserved, cannot be long endured; and the weakening of the social side of religion in the outside world will tend to weaken it in the family also; and the weakening of the religious bond between members of the same household, beginning at that early age at which we first think that we are thinking for ourselves, will leave the family reduced to the insecure bond of affection and sentiment. Thus, when religion comes to be more and more an individual matter, and is no longer a family tie; when it becomes a matter of voluntary association on one day a week when the weather is neither too good nor too bad, and of a traditional and more and more meaningless verbiage in the pulpit and at times upon the political platform; when it ceases to inform the whole of life; then a vacuum is discovered, and the beliefs in religion will be gradually supplanted by a belief in the State. That part of the social life which is independent of the State will be diminished to the more trivial. The necessity will appear for a common belief in *something* to fill the place of religion in the community; and the liberals will find themselves surrendering more and more of the individual freedom which was the basis of their doctrine.

Let me return for a moment to the terms in which I put the first of my alternatives; that is,

> where the State itself professes allegiance to a particular religion or religious denomination, this religion may be affirmed, and taught, in all the educational institutions controlled by the State; and the teaching will be in conformity with the doctrines of this religion.

Now there are obvious practical difficulties here, the first of which is that such a system is patently out of the question in any actual English-speaking country. We have a bias in favour of freedom: and we are not racially or religiously sufficiently homogeneous. But where such homogeneity is found, there are incidental dangers to the spiritual life of a people upon which I shall not dilate. The more general dangers are three: that the State shall control the Church, or fashion its own Church; that the Church shall control the State; or that the citizen shall think of himself as owing allegiance, on the same plane, to two States. For the term 'religion' is just as slippery as 'education', or 'democracy', or a host of other terms: we tend to mean one thing in one context and another in another, and to think that because we use the same word we are indicating the same thing. When we talk of Church and State we are contrasting two institutions, and the Church is something more, and something different from a secular institution. We are ignoring the religious aspect of the Church; and religion, just because it comprehends everything, cannot be compared with anything.

There is another complication which I must introduce at this point. You may remember that I started by criticizing the three aims of education which I took over, as a point of departure, from Dr. Joad. I suggested that whereas 'education for citizenship' might come to mean something too precise and restricted to the standards of the moment, education for 'the development of latent powers' was dangerously vague; and that it was for another authority than the State to instruct us in the cultivation and discipline of moral, intellectual, and spiritual powers with which the State was not concerned. An excessive interference and control by the State, in the answer to the question 'What is a good citizen?' and a State regulation of the discipline calculated to produce good citizens, would produce only *conformity*. An excessive interference and control by a Church, in the answer to the question 'What is a good man?' might also produce mere conformity. For there are many aspects of the good life, both for the individual and for society, with which the Church is not directly concerned. The direct question to which the church of any religion must provide an answer is 'What is necessary for salvation?' Several churches, at various times and places, have been so sure that nothing was necessary *but* salvation, that a good deal of harm has come of it: for instance, the destruction of the Library of Alexandria by the Moslem invaders, the spoliation of shrines and casting down of images in the Protestant Reformation, and the use of torture and appalling forms of death as a deterrent to heresy. On the other hand, in past ages the churches of all countries have been the centres for the arts; the religions of Europe and Asia have provided the motive for the greatest works of art of these continents; and the civilizations of Europe and Asia would be inconceivable without their religious basis. Yet civilization, and the development of higher forms of culture, can only be considered, from the religious point of view, as by-products. The fact that we do not get them except through belief in a religion does not imply that any church, or any minister of religion, is necessarily competent to pronounce in all questions of art—as inspection of some modern religious edifices will attest.

It should by now be apparent why I suggested beforehand, in turning to the question of the place of religion in education, that all of the possibilities I listed were unsatisfactory. It is at least clear that in a society in which the population is not of only one religion, or, within one religion, is divided into sects—and this is the kind of society for which we have to legislate in English-speaking countries—one or another compromise must be practised, and each society or community must find out for itself which kind of compromise is least unsatisfactory for its own religion. So that in such countries any theory of education which the framer designs to be realizable must stop short at the point beyond which religious differences cannot be ignored. Unless we can get complete agreement about religious truth—that is, the ultimate truth about Man—we must not expect to be able to agree upon an ideal system of education which can be put into practice. Many situations in life have to be dealt with by compromise, and we must not repine over this misfortune of the human condition. But I think that it is very important, when we are forced by circumstances to stop short of the proper terminus of our speculations, to be aware of what we are doing; in respect to the present subject matter, not to pretend that a theory of education can be complete which excludes the ultimate religious problems—and I have said that 'What is Man?' is one of these—and which attempts to delimit for the theory of education an area within which religion can be ignored.

I am now, I hope, in a position to remark that the inquiry into 'the place of religious teaching in education' with which I have been occupying myself for some minutes is really unimportant for the purposes which I set myself in these discourses. Only, it is a problem which has to be inquired into first, before we can see how and why it is unimportant in this context. In my 'aims of education' it is not the place of religion in education, but the place of education in religion, that is the vital issue. I began with stating three aims of education on which I hoped that we should all agree, and then attempted to show first that each of these aims was involved in the others, and that each both extended and qualified the meaning of the others. I tried to show, after this, that the pursuit of the meaning of these three aims leads us beyond the frontiers of the area which we should like to fence off as that of education, and forces us into the difficult territory of social and political philosophy, ethics, and finally metaphysics and theology. So that until we all come to agree in our theology, our agreement on educational questions can be only an agreement on what is possible and desirable for a particular society under the peculiar conditions of its place, time, and composition. And in our theoretical discussion of education we should try to make clear to ourselves and to others what philosophy is behind our opinions.

I do not want to leave you with the impression that I think we should postpone our discussions of education, or our attempts to improve present systems and correct their faults, until we have come to an agreement on ultimate problems. Nor do I presume that if we all came to hold the same philosophical and religious views we should suddenly all find ourselves in agreement as to how to run our schools and universities. We should simply have got to a point at which the possibilities of confusion and misunderstanding and conflict would be minimized. There would remain many questions to which philosophy and theology could give no direct answer, or to which they would give a variety of possible answers; and there would still be a vast field for that disagreement, argument, and experiment which are necessary for activity and improvement.

Let me now, as I draw to a close, try to sum up the several conclusions to which I have come on the way. First, that 'good citizenship' cannot be wholly limited to the definition of it provided by a government, or the doctrines of any particular political philosophy. Second, that the question 'What is the development of latent powers of the individual?' or the question 'How is man as man to be improved?' cannot be answered without reference to theology, although much is included in 'improvement' which is not immediately in the province of theology. So, while we have found that we must consult our political philosophers for the elucidation they can give of our second aim of education, and that we must consult our theologians for help in elucidating the third, and our theologians who are also political philosophers for whatever they have to say on both questions together, we find that none of them covers the whole area to which each aim applies, and we are forced to reopen the question.

We have found that the two aims imply each other, just as both are implied in the first. We can say that we agree that every human being should, ideally, be educated to do the best of which he is capable by his neighbours and himself. He should, furthermore, be educated to be able to decide between conflicting claims: for we are, in practice, often faced with the necessity for sacrificing self-interest—not selfishness, but a high self-interest—to social claims, or of sacrificing social obligations to the needs of our own essential self. There are the claims represented by the State, and the claims represented by the Church; but there are, furthermore, the claims represented by our own being. If I feel ready to write a poem, and I therefore decline to address a meeting on behalf of some good cause, or prepare a paper for an important weekend conference, what is the outcome? If the poem turns out to be a good one, I feel justified; if it is a failure, I feel guilty. The success is always uncertain; and as for the failure, I am thinking of instances in which one could have been certain, in sacrificing the writing of the poem, of being engaged otherwise in doing something at least moderately useful. And if it is difficult to decide for ourselves, it is often impossible to judge for others. Was Thoreau a good citizen when he retired to Walden? Many a man has pursued a course which seemed folly to his family, or which appeared antisocial, or which meant pain and sacrifice for others, and we denounce him or praise him afterwards according to results which could never have been predicted. So I think we must allow a place after all to individual choice in 'the development of latent powers', although with all the qualifications with which we have now loaded the phrase.

There is, however, another lane up which I must chase a hare before coming to my conclusion. So far, our aims have been for the individual: to train him to become the best that he is capable of becoming. We have been concerned only with the present, not with the past or the future. Now I suggest that one aim of education should be concerned with another obligation besides that towards the persons to be taught. If we consider only the latter, our curriculum may vary with every wind of doctrine; our notions of what is a good way of earning a living, of what is good citizenship, and of what is good individual development, may be at the mercy of the prevailing mood of one generation, or the caprice of individual educators. It should be an aim of education to maintain the continuity of our culture–and neither continuity, nor a respect for the past, implies standing still. More than ever, we should look to education today to preserve us from the error of pure contemporaneity. We look to institutions of education to maintain a knowledge and understanding of the past. And the past has to be reinterpreted for each generation, for each generation brings its own prejudices and fresh misunderstandings. All this may be comprehended in the term history; but history includes the study of the great dead languages and of the past of modern languages, including our own. Particularly, indeed, our own; for we need to understand the way in which our words have been used in the past, how they have developed and altered their meanings, in order to understand how we are using them ourselves. And to preserve the wisdom of the past, we need to value it for its own sake, not simply to defend it on the ground of its usefulness. To support religion on the ground of its usefulness is obvious error; for the question, of what use is man to God, is more important than the question, of what use is God to man; and there is an analogy–though I admit the danger of drawing such an analogy with temporal affairs–in our relation to our culture. For if we estimate the wisdom and experience and art of the past only in terms of its usefulness to us, we are in danger of limiting the meaning of 'usefulness', and of limiting the meaning of 'us' to those who are now alive. What I wish to maintain is a point of view from which it appears more important–if we have to choose, and perhaps we do have to choose–that a small number of people should be educated well, and others left with only a rudimentary education, than that everybody should receive a share of an inferior quality of education, whereby we delude ourselves into thinking that whatever there can be the most of, must be the best. And what I plead for is what Matthew Arnold spoke of as 'the knowledge of the best that has been thought and said in the world' (and, I might add, the best that has been done in the world, and that has been created in the arts in the world); that this knowledge of history, in the widest sense, should not be reserved to a small body of experts–reserved to them and parcelled out among them–but that it should be the common possession of those who have passed through the higher grades of nonspecialized education; that it might well form, for most of them, the foundation for many of the more modern studies which now tend to be substituted for it.

We may now, having taken account of the aims of education and pursued the definition as far as we could, proceed to inquire what is the use of the sort of conclusion we arrive at. We find that we have given no definition of education, that in fact education does not appear to be definable. The most that we can do is to list a number of the things that education might be expected to do, and try to show that each of these, if it is to be called education, must imply the rest. They are several of the purposes which education has been made to serve; we have been able to arrive at definitions, of a sort, of some of these purposes; and although we cannot define education *simpliciter*, our awareness of the mutual implication of its several purposes gives us a feeling of an identity of the word which is similar to the feeling I have professed to have of identity among the several uses of the word *runcible*. We must continue, however, to speak of 'education' when we mean one of several possible uses of the word; and this felt identity is what makes it impossible for us to substitute, for the sake of clarity, several different words.

The final question is, 'What is the use of such inquiries: that is, does it make any difference to education in practice whether we speculate about the meaning of the word or not?' Men have been training their children ever since they were men, and indeed before it: I do not know at what precise point in the scale of living creatures the training of the young may be said to begin. The content of education and its form have varied according to the organization of the society in and for which the young have been trained; a long tradition and many educational institutions preceded the time at which the question 'What is education?' needed to be asked. Or rather, we ask the question about the purpose of an activity at some time after we have begun to practise it; and we have found that the question has to be asked again and again, because the activity itself alters from generation to generation. But the machinery of education, which has now become vast and complicated almost the world over, has to be kept going all the time. Many changes and developments are due to accidents, to response to local and immediate circumstances; some are due to the deliberate purpose of individual educators—right or wrong; some to the influence of a book, such as Rousseau's *Emile* (and Rousseau was a literary dabbler like myself); some to political theory or theological doctrine; some to wisdom, some to folly, and some to circumstances beyond our control. But when we set out to define education, what are we trying to do? We are not trying to compose a lexical definition—that is, the customary use of a word. We are attempting to isolate the common element in a great number of kinds of training, pursued for different ends, in very different civilizations. We are attempting, that is, to devise a master key for a number of different locks. But we are also attempting to find a stipulative definition: we are not merely trying to say what the word education means—that is, has meant to those people whom we consider qualified to use it—but what true education should be. We are aiming at a real rather than a nominal definition, and are in effect trying to persuade people to accept a definition of our own. But our motive for attempting a definition may spring from our objection to the practice of education which we have endured or observed, or to the theories of other people of what education is. Since I have insisted on the fact that behind every theory of education we find, implicit or explicit, philosophical and theological, as well as sociological premises, it might be thought the question is one only for philosophers, and not for those engaged in teaching and the administration of educational institutions. But the latter have a fund of experience, and, if they are wise men, a store of wisdom, about education, which only those who have actually made teaching their vocation can have. It seems to me that it is the task of educators to think and to write about education, but to clarify for themselves the social, philosophical and theological presuppositions which underlie their generalizations; and it is for the pure theoretician, the philosopher or theologian, to refer his theories to the educator—the man who has had experience of the difficulties of teaching anybody anything. It is, incidentally, for the legislator, when he is moved by aught but political expediency, to consult both, as well as to do a little thinking for himself.

It is obvious that no lexical definition of education can answer the question 'What is education?' since all that a dictionary can do is to tell us the principal ways in which the word has been used in the past, and up to the date at which the lexicographer compiled his account of the word, by those writers whose authority he respects. While we are aware of a relation among these several definitions of the uses of the word, we seem unable to get any one primary definition, which all these secondary definitions will imply. The definition we are seeking is one which involves judgments of value; it will therefore be one upon which we cannot all agree, so cannot possibly be a definition in the dictionary sense. (Incidentally, people have been very far from agreeing upon a definition of the word 'definition.') As for the list of aims, whether it be of three or more, and whether we introduce subdivisions or not, there are several qualifications to be made. It is always possible that one or more of the purposes listed by a writer may be wrong, or wholly unacceptable to others; it is possible that what is in fact the same purpose may be expressed by different writers in quite different terms; and it is always possible that the list ought to be longer. We all try, of course, to reduce it to as few as possible: that is one of the rules of the game. But just as the meaning of the word education has developed in the past, and may be expected to develop and change further in the future, so it is possible that in some future and unpredictable situation the purposes of education will have to be formulated anew, and also that new purposes may appear which cannot be reduced to terms of those already recognized.

It may be observed, also, that the more clear and distinct we make our ideas on the subject, the less is the likelihood of agreement on what these aims or purposes are. The more definite your views, the fewer people will be found to accept them. Most people will accept the assertion that education involves some kind of moral training; fewer will accept the assertion that it involves religious training; and of those who accept the principle of religious training, fewer still will agree on how far it should go and how dogmatic it should be. We may agree that the educational question can be satisfactorily answered 'when we get our metaphysics, ethnics, psychology, theology and politics straight enough to think straight about it.' But this is a date, I suspect, at the other end of infinity. The prospect of the sages of any one of these disciplines agreeing amongst themselves seems remote; the prospect of the practitioners of these several disciplines agreeing with each other, and upon the relative contributions of their sciences to the perfecting of education, seems remoter still.

We are all, in fact, trying to persuade other people: that is, we appeal to their emotions, and often indeed to their prejudices, as well as to their reason; and the best we can do is to see that *as well as* (to our reason) does not become *instead of* (to our reason). We can at least *try* to understand our own motives, passions, and prejudices, so as to be conscious of what we are doing when we appeal to those of others. This is very difficult, because our own prejudice and emotional bias always seem to us so rational. We are perpetually engaged in pointing out the extent to which other people's reasoning is deflected by their sentiments. I am quite aware that I have been trying to persuade, though I may not be quite sure of what. But although I should be discouraged if nobody agreed with anything I have said, I should be thoroughly alarmed if everybody agreed; because a statement upon which everyone can agree, in the discussion of topics such as these, is pretty certain not to mean much. I hope, however, that my main motive has been to unsettle your minds, rather than to impose a theory; and while I have gone on defining, I have not been thinking of convincing, though you may have been thinking of your next cocktail party.

WHAT DANTE MEANS TO ME[1]

May I explain first why I have chosen, not to deliver a lecture about Dante, but to talk informally about his influence upon myself? What might appear egotism, in doing this, I present as modesty; and the modesty which it pretends to be is merely prudence. I am in no way a Dante scholar; and my general knowledge of Italian is such, that on this occasion, out of respect to the audience and to Dante himself, I shall refrain from quoting him in Italian. And I do not feel that I have anything more to contribute, on the subject of Dante's poetry, than I put, years ago, into a brief essay. As I explained in the original preface to that essay, I read Dante only with a prose translation beside the text. Forty years ago I began to puzzle out the Divine Comedy in this way; and when I thought I had grasped the meaning of a passage which especially delighted me, I committed it to memory; so that, for some years, I was able to recite a large part of one canto or another to myself, lying in bed or on a railway journey. Heaven knows what it would have sounded like, had I recited it aloud; but it was by this means that I steeped myself in Dante's poetry. And now it is twenty years since I set down all that my meagre attainments qualified me to say about Dante. But I thought it not uninteresting to myself, and possibly to others, to try to record in what my own debt to Dante consists. I do not think I can explain everything, even to myself; but as I still, after forty years, regard his poetry as the most persistent and deepest influence upon my own verse, I should like to establish at least some of the reasons for it. Perhaps confessions by poets, of what Dante has meant to them, may even contribute something to the appreciation of Dante himself. And finally, it is the only contribution that I can make.

[1] A talk given at the Italian Institute, London, on July 4th, 1950.

The greatest debts are not always the most evident; at least, there are different kinds of debt. The kind of debt that I owe to Dante is the kind which goes on accumulating, the kind which is not the debt of one period or another of one's life. Of some poets I can say I learned a great deal from them at a particular stage. Of Jules Laforgue, for instance, I can say that he was the first to teach me how to speak, to teach me the poetic possibilities of my own idiom of speech. Such early influences, the influences which, so to speak, first introduce one to oneself, are, I think, due to an impression which is in one aspect, the recognition of a temperament akin to one's own, and in another aspect the discovery of a form of expression which gives a clue to the discovery of one's own form. These are not two things, but two aspects of the same thing. But the poet who can do this for a young writer, is unlikely to be one of the great masters. The latter are too exalted and too remote. They are like distant ancestors who have been almost deified; whereas the smaller poet, who has directed one's first steps, is more like an admired elder brother.

Then, among influences, there are the poets from whom one has learned some one thing, perhaps of capital importance to oneself, though not necessarily the greatest contribution these poets have made. I think that from Baudelaire I learned first, a precedent for the poetical possibilities, never developed by any poet writing in my own language, of the more sordid aspects of the modern metropolis, of the possibility of fusion between the sordidly realistic and the phantasmagoric, the possibility of the juxtaposition of the matter-of-fact and the fantastic. From him, as from Laforgue, I learned that the sort of material that I had, the sort of experience that an adolescent had had, in an industrial city in America, could be the material for poetry; and that the source of new poetry might be found in what had been regarded hitherto as the impossible, the sterile, the intractably unpoetic. That, in fact, the business of the poet was to make poetry out of the unexplored resources of the unpoetical; that the poet, in fact, was committed by his profession to turn the unpoetical into poetry. A great poet can give a younger poet everything that he has to give him, in a very few lines. It may be that I am indebted to Baudelaire chiefly for half a dozen lines out of the whole of *Fleurs du Mal*; and that his significance for me is summed up in the lines:

> *Fourmillante Cité, cité pleine de rêves,*
> *Où le spectre en plein jour raccroche le passant . . .*

I knew what *that* meant, because I had lived it before I knew that I wanted to turn it into verse on my own account.

I may seem to you to be very far from Dante. But I cannot give you any approximation of what Dante has done for me, without speaking of what other poets have done for me. When I have written about Baudelaire, or Dante, or any other poet who has had a capital importance in my own development, I have written *because* that poet has meant so much to me, but not about myself, but *about* that poet and his poetry. That is, the first impulse to write about a great poet is one of gratitude; but the reasons for which one is grateful may play a very small part in a critical appreciation of that poet.

One has other debts, innumerable debts, to poets, of another kind. There are poets who have been at the back of one's mind, or perhaps consciously there, when one has had some particular problem to settle, for which something they have written suggests the method. There are those from whom one has consciously borrowed, adapting a line of verse to a different language or period or context. There are those who remain in one's mind as having set the standard for a particular poetic virtue, as Villon for honesty, and Sappho for having fixed a particular emotion in the right and the minimum number of words, once and for all. There are also the great masters, to whom one slowly grows up. When I was young I felt much more at ease with the lesser Elizabethan dramatists than with Shakespeare: the former were, so to speak, playmates nearer my own size. One test of the great masters, of whom Shakespeare is one, is that the appreciation of their poetry is a lifetime's task, because at every stage of maturing—and that should be one's whole life—you are able to understand them better. Among these are Shakespeare, Dante, Homer and Virgil.

I have ranged over some varieties of 'influence' in order to approach an indication, by contrast, of what Dante has meant to me. Certainly I have borrowed lines from him, in the attempt to reproduce, or rather to arouse in the reader's mind the memory, of some Dantesque scene, and thus establish a relationship between the medieval inferno and modern life. Readers of my *Waste Land* will perhaps remember that the vision of my city clerks trooping over London Bridge from the railway station to their offices evoked the reflection 'I had not thought death had undone so many'; and that in another place I deliberately modified a line of Dante by altering it—'sighs, short and infrequent, were exhaled.' And I gave the references in my notes, in order to make the reader who recognized the allusion, know that I meant him to recognize it, and know that he would have missed the point if he did not recognize it. Twenty years after writing *The Waste Land*, I wrote, in *Little Gidding*, a passage which is intended to be the nearest equivalent to a canto of the Inferno or the Purgatorio, in style as well as content, that I could achieve. The intention, of course, was the same as with my allusions to Dante in *The Waste Land*: to present to the mind of the reader a parallel, by means of contrast, between the Inferno and the Purgatorio, which Dante visited and a hallucinated scene after an air-raid. But the method is different: here I was debarred from quoting or adapting at length—I borrowed and adapted freely only a few phrases—because I was *imitating*. My first problem was to find an approximation to the *terza rima* without rhyming. English is less copiously provided with rhyming words than Italian; and those rhymes we have are in a way more emphatic. The rhyming words call too much attention to themselves: Italian is the one language known to me in which exact rhyme can always achieve its effect—and what the effect of rhyme is, is for the neurologist rather than the poet to investigate—without the risk of obtruding itself. I therefore adopted, for my purpose, a simple alternation of unrhymed masculine and feminine terminations, as the nearest way of giving the light effect of the rhyme in Italian. In saying this, I am not attempting to lay down a law, but merely explaining how I was directed in a particular situation. I think that rhymed *terza rima* is probably less unsatisfactory for translation of the Divine Comedy than is blank verse. For, unfortunately for this purpose, a different metre is a different mode of thought; it is a different kind of *punctuation*, for the emphases and the breath pauses do not come in the same place. Dante *thought* in *terza rima*, and a poem should be translated as nearly as possible in the same thought-form as the original. So that, in a translation into blank verse, something is lost; though on the other hand, when I read a *terza rima* translation of the Divine Comedy and come to some passage of which I remember the original pretty closely, I am always worried in anticipation, by the inevitable shifts and twists which I know the translator will be obliged to make, in order to fit Dante's words into English rhyme. And no verse seems to demand greater literalness in translation than Dante's, because no poet convinces one more completely that the word he has used is the word he wanted, and that no other will do.

I do not know whether the substitute for rhyme that I used in the passage referred to would be tolerable for a very long original poem in English: but I do know that I myself should not find the rest of my life long enough time in which to write it. For one of the interesting things I learnt in trying to imitate Dante in English, was its extreme difficulty. This section of a poem—not the length of one canto of the Divine Comedy—cost me far more time and trouble and vexation than any passage of the same length that I have ever written. It was not simply that I was limited to the Dantesque type of imagery, simile and figure of speech. It was chiefly that in this very bare and austere style, in which every word has to be 'functional', the slightest vagueness or imprecision is immediately noticeable. The language has to be very direct; the line, and the single word, must be completely disciplined to the purpose of the whole; and, when you are using simple words and simple phrases, any repetition of the most common idiom, or of the most frequently needed word, becomes a glaring blemish.

I am not saying that *terza rima* is to be ruled out of original English verse composition; though I believe that to the modern ear—that is, the ear trained during this century, and therefore accustomed to much greater exercise in the possibilities of unrhymed verse—a modern long poem in a set rhymed form is more likely to sound monotonous as well as artificial, than it did to the ear of a hundred years ago. But I am sure that it is only possible in a long poem, if the poet is borrowing only the form, and not attempting to remind the reader of Dante in every line and phrase. There is one poem in the nineteenth century which, at moments, seems to contradict this. This is the *Triumph of Life*. I should have felt called upon today to refer to Shelley in any case, because Shelley is the English poet, more than all others, upon whom the influence of Dante was remarkable. It seems to me that Shelley confirms also my impression that the influence of Dante, where it is really powerful, is a *cumulative* influence: that is, the older you grow, the stronger the domination becomes. The *Triumph of Life*, a poem which is Shelley's greatest tribute to Dante, was the last of his great poems. I think it was also the greatest. It was left unfinished; it breaks off abruptly in the middle of a line; and one wonders whether even Shelley could have carried it to successful completion. Now the influence of Dante is observable earlier; most evident in the *Ode to the West Wind*, in which, at the very beginning, the image of the leaves whirling in the wind

Like stricken ghosts from an enchanter fleeing

would have been impossible but for the Inferno—in which the various manifestations of *wind*, and the various sensations of *air*, are as important as are the aspects of *light* in the Paradiso. In *The Triumph of Life* however I do not think that Shelley was setting himself to aim at such a close approximation to the spareness of Dante as I was; he had left open for himself all of his copious resources of English poetical speech. Nevertheless, because of a natural affinity with the poetic imagination of Dante, a saturation in the poetry (and I need not remind you that Shelley knew Italian well, and had a wide and thorough knowledge of all Italian poetry up to his time) his mind is inspired to some of the greatest and most Dantesque lines in English. I must quote one passage which made an indelible impression upon me over forty-five years ago:

Struck to the heart by this sad pageantry,
Half to myself I said—'And what is this?
Whose shape is that within the car? and why—'

I would have added—'is all here amiss?'
But a voice answered—'Life!'—I turned, and knew
(O Heaven, have mercy on such wretchedness!)

That what I thought was an old root which grew
To strange distortion out of the hill side,
Was indeed one of those deluded crew,

And that the grass, which methought hung so wide
And white, was but his thin discoloured hair,
And that the holes he vainly sought to hide,

Were or had been eyes:—'If thou canst, forbear
To join the dance, which I had well forborne!',
Said the grim Feature (of my thought aware).

'I will unfold that which to this deep scorn
Led me and my companions, and relate
The progress of the pageant since the morn;

If thirst of knowledge shall not then abate,
Follow it thou even to the night, but I
Am weary.'—Then like one who with the weight

Of his own words is staggered, wearily
He paused; and ere he could resume, I cried:
'First, who art thou?'—'Before thy memory,

I feared, loved, hated, suffered, did and died,
And if the spark with which Heaven lit my spirit
Had been with purer nutriment supplied,

Corruption would not now thus much inherit
Of what was once Rousseau,—nor this disguise
Stain that which ought to have disdained to wear it . . .

Well, this is better than I could do. But I quote it, as one of the supreme tributes to Dante in English; for it testifies to what Dante has done, both for the style and for the soul, of a great English poet. And incidentally, a very interesting comment on Rousseau. It would be interesting, but otiose, to pursue the evidence of Shelley's debt to Dante further; it is sufficient, to those who know the source, to quote the first three of the prefatory lines to *Epipsychidion*—

My Song, I fear that thou wilt find but few
Who fitly shall conceive thy reasoning,
Of such hard matter dost thou entertain.

I think I have already made clear, however, that the important debt to Dante does not lie in a poet's borrowings, or adaptations from Dante; nor is it one of those debts which are incurred only at a particular stage in another poet's development. Nor is it found in those passages in which one has taken him as a model. The important debt does not occur in relation to the number of places in one's writings to which a critic can point a finger, and say, here and there he wrote something which he could not have written unless he had had Dante in mind. Nor do I wish to speak now of any debt which one may owe to the thought of Dante, to his view of life, or to the philosophy and theology which give shape and content to the Divine Comedy. That is another, though by no means unrelated question. Of what one learns, and goes on learning, from Dante I should like to make three points.

The first is, that of the very few poets of similar stature there is none, not even Virgil, who has been a more attentive student of the *art* of poetry, or a more scrupulous, painstaking and *conscious* practitioner of the *craft*. Certainly no English poet can be compared with him in this respect, for the more conscious craftsmen—and I am thinking primarily of Milton—have been much more limited poets, and therefore more limited in their craft also. To realize more and more what this means, through the years of one's life, is itself a moral lesson; but I draw a further lesson from it which is a moral lesson too. The whole study and practice of Dante seems to me to teach that the poet should be the servant of his language, rather than the master of it. This sense of responsibility is one of the marks of the *classical* poet, in the sense of 'classical' which I have tried to define elsewhere, in speaking of Virgil. Of some great poets, and of some great English poets especially, one can say that they were privileged by their genius to *abuse* the English language, to develop an idiom so peculiar and even eccentric, that it could be of no use to later poets. Dante seems to me to have a place in Italian literature—which, in this respect, only Shakespeare has in ours; that is, they give body to the soul of the language, conforming themselves, the one more and the other less consciously, to what they divined to be its possibilities. And Shakespeare himself takes liberties which only his genius justifies; liberties which Dante, with an equal genius, does not take. To pass on to posterity one's own language, more highly developed, more refined, and more precise than it was before one wrote it, that is the highest possible achievement of the poet as poet. Of course, a really supreme poet makes poetry also more difficult for his successors, but the simple fact of his supremacy, and the price a literature must pay, for having a Dante or a Shakespeare, is that it can have only *one*. Later poets must find something else to do, and be content if the things left to do are lesser things. But I am not speaking of what a supreme poet, one of those few without whom the current speech of a people with a great language would not be what it is, does for later poets, or of what he prevents them from doing, but of what he does for everybody after him who speaks that language, whose mother tongue it is, whether they are poets, philosophers, statesmen or railway porters.

That is one lesson: that the great master of a language should be the great servant of it. The second lesson of Dante—and it is one which no poet, in any language known to me, can teach—is the lesson of *width of emotional range*. Perhaps it could be best expressed under the figure of the spectrum, or of the gamut. Employing this figure, I may say that the great poet should not only perceive and distinguish more clearly than other men, the colours or sounds within the range of ordinary vision or hearing; he should perceive vibrations beyond the range of ordinary men, and be able to make men see and hear more at each end than they could ever see without his help. We have for instance in English literature great religious poets, but they are, by comparison with Dante, *specialists*. That is all they can do. And Dante, because he could do everything else, is for that reason the greatest 'religious' poet, though to call him a 'religious poet' would be to abate his universality. The Divine Comedy expresses everything in the way of emotion, between depravity's despair and the beatific vision, that man is capable of experiencing. It is therefore a constant reminder to the poet, of the obligation to explore, to find words for the inarticulate, to capture those feelings which people can hardly even feel, because they have no words for them; and at the same time, a reminder that the explorer beyond the frontiers of ordinary consciousness will only be able to return and report to his fellow-citizens, if he has all the time a firm grasp upon the realities with which they are already acquainted.

These two achievements of Dante are not to be thought of as separate or separable. The task of the poet, in making people comprehend the incomprehensible, demands immense resources of language; and in developing the language, enriching the meaning of words and showing how much words can do, he is making possible a much greater range of emotion and perception for other men, because he gives them the speech in which more can be expressed. I only suggest as an instance what Dante did for his own language—and for ours, since we have taken the word and anglicized it—by the verb *trasumanar*.

What I have been saying just now is not irrelevant to the fact—for to me it appears an incontestable fact—that Dante is, beyond all other poets of our continent, the most *European*. He is the least provincial—and yet that statement must be immediately protected by saying that he did not become the 'least provincial' by ceasing to be local. No one is more local; one never forgets that there is much in Dante's poetry which escapes any reader whose native language is not Italian; but I think that the foreigner is less *aware* of any residuum that must for ever escape him, than any of us is in reading any other master of a language which is not our own. The Italian of Dante is somehow *our* language from the moment we begin to try to read it; and the lessons of craft, of speech and of exploration of sensibility are lessons which any European can take to heart and try to apply in his own tongue.

See P. 377
Edmund Wilson
"The Bit Between My Teeth"

THE LITERATURE OF POLITICS[1]

Not today, for the first time, but for some time past, have I been aware how very rash it was of me to accept your invitation to address this Literary Luncheon: my acceptance is only one more illustration of a truth that I should have learned from experience, that one can face nearly any danger intrepidly, and even court it wantonly, so long as it is far enough off. My foolhardiness, on this occasion, was twofold. While I do not suppose that everyone in this room is an accomplished public speaker, I take it for granted that those who are not, are at least seasoned listeners, with pretty high standards of what they expect in the way of oratory. And a man of letters, far from being thereby licensed to the platform and the rostrum, is more likely than not to be a poor speaker, relatively at ease—but only relatively—when he has prepared, as I have today, not only his thoughts but his words. Second, I was rash in consenting to appear in an unfamiliar role and context. That, of course, may have increased the size of my audience: you are, very likely, at this moment experiencing the thrill of a crowd gathered to watch a man take a very high dive, when the rumour has been put about that he does not know how to swim. I hope you will be disappointed: but I do not know myself whether or not, after the splash has subsided, my head will emerge from the water.

Some excitement and misunderstanding may have arisen from the title originally advertised, which led a columnist in a daily newspaper to exclaim: 'Mr. Eliot, who writes his plays in verse, is turning to politics. He has kept well away from them up to now.' Well, I intend to be just as political, and not a

[1] This lecture was delivered at a Literary Luncheon organized by the London Conservative Union on April 19th, 1955.

jot more so, than I have been in some of my prose writings which perhaps the writer, so appreciative of my plays, has overlooked.

The title first given is one which I suggested as a good subject for somebody—without specifying myself. Rather late in the day I realized that the title had come home to roost and that I must push it off the roost. I am reminded of an experience some years ago when I agreed to give a lecture in Nice. In correspondence with the President of the society which I was to address, I remarked that, not knowing which of two kinds of audience to expect, I found myself, for the choice of a subject, between Scylla and Charybdis. Before I had made up my mind what to talk about, it was announced in Nice that I was to speak on the subject of Scylla and Charybdis. After a moment's consternation I thought—And why not? Almost any topic can be dealt with under that heading. *Scylla and Charybdis* is delightfully general, and arouses curiosity by its vagueness. *The Relation of Political Philosophy to the Practice of Politics*, on the other hand, was alarmingly precise. It is a subject to demand all the learning, profundity and torrential eloquence of such a philosopher as Mr. Isaiah Berlin. As for me, I am not competing with such authorities. I am merely a man of letters who believes that the questions he raises may sometimes be of interest, even if the answers he can give are negligible. And as a man of letters, I have never taken any part in politics other than that of a voter—a walking-on part, and that of a reader—a sitting-down part.

So let me approach my subject by asking: what is the literature of Conservatism? That is to say, what are the 'classic' writings in the English language, with which any thoughtful Conservative is presumed to have some familiarity, writings by authors whose work is supposed to yield some understanding of what Conservatism is? There are four names which we could all, without any prompting, repeat in chorus, for they constantly turn up together. They lead off in the bibliographical note to that admirable little book *Conservatism* written by Lord Hugh Cecil, as he was then, in 1912 for the Home University Library. They are, of course, the names of Bolingbroke, Burke, Coleridge and Disraeli.

Now, could one assemble four men, in one field of thought, more dissimilar to each other than these? The one thing they obviously have in common is that each in his way was a master of prose, whose work can no more be ignored by the student of English literature than by the student of politics. Each of these men had a sense of style—and that is something more than merely a trick of knowing how to write. This is all to the good, that the Conservative tradition should be also a tradition of good writing; but it may seem irrelevant. When we consider Bolingbroke, he is hardly an example of that devotion to Christian belief and Christian morals that Lord Hugh Cecil quite rightly called for. Burke is certainly a Christian thinker; Coleridge was a distinguished theologian as well as philosopher; Disraeli also deserves a pass degree, though churchmanship is the one point on which I feel more sympathy with Mr. Gladstone. As for their politics, the situations in which the three who practised politics found themselves, were very different. Bolingbroke, in fact, is pre-Conservative, if we agree with those who derive Conservatism itself only from a fusion of Tory and Whig elements, due largely to the effect of the French Revolution upon the mind of Burke. Burke, as has often been observed, uttered his most important statements of Conservative doctrine in the course of current controversy; Disraeli delivered himself through his novels as well as in Parliament. As for Coleridge, he was rather a man of my own type, differing from myself chiefly in being immensely more learned, more industrious, and endowed with a more powerful and subtle mind.

So we remark that, with three of these writers, their philosophy was nourished on their political experience. The fourth was a philosopher with no political experience. What are we to make of this diversity, and what common principles can be elicited from the work of such different men, writing under such different conditions? I am inclined to believe it a good thing that we should find the question difficult to answer. If, in my attempt to give grounds for my belief, you find me descending to platitude and commonplace, I hope you will attribute it to my simplicity and inexperience; if, on the other hand, you convict me of uttering nonsense, I ask for no quarter at all.

I venture to put forward the suggestion that political thinking, that is, thinking that concerns itself with the permanent principles, if any, underlying a party name, can follow two contrasted lines of development. At the beginning may be a body of doctrine, perhaps a canonical work; and a band of devoted people set out to disseminate and popularize this doctrine through its emotional appeal to the interested and the disinterested; and then, as a political party, endeavour to realize a programme based on the doctrine. Before arriving at the position of governing, they have envisaged some final state of society of which their doctrines give the outline. The theory has altogether preceded the practice.

But political ideas may come into being by an opposite process. A political party may find that it has had a history, before it is fully aware of or agreed upon its own permanent tenets; it may have arrived at its actual formation through a succession of metamorphoses and adaptations, during which some issues have been superannuated and new issues have arisen. What its fundamental tenets are, will probably be found only by careful examination of its behaviour throughout its history and by examination of what its more thoughtful and philosophic minds have said on its behalf; and only accurate historical knowledge and judicious analysis will be able to discriminate between the permanent and the transitory; between those doctrines and principles which it must ever, and in all circumstances, maintain, or manifest itself a fraud, and those called forth by special circumstances, which are only intelligible and justifiable in the light of those circumstances.

Of the two, the latter type seems to me the more likely to correspond to that preference of the organic over the mechanical that Burke maintained: but each has its peculiar dangers.

I do not propose to plunge into the controversies of historical determinism. Determinism has a strong emotional appeal: curiously enough, it can appeal to the same type of mind as that which believes in the unlimited possibilities of planning. Determinism seems to give great encouragement, and at times access of force, to those who can convince themselves that what they want to happen is going to happen anyway, and to those who like to feel that they are going with the tide: and we have all heard, now and again, that freedom is to be found only in the acceptance of necessity—though it is also natural to the human mind to suspect that there is a catch in this somewhere. But it should also be obvious to everyone from his personal experience, that there is no formula for infallible prediction; that everything we do will have some unforeseen consequences; that often our best justified ventures end in disaster, and that sometimes our most irrational blunders have the most happy results; that every reform leads to new abuses which could not have been predicted but which do not necessarily justify us in saying that the reform should not have been carried out; that we must constantly adapt ourselves to the new and unexpected; and that we move always, if not in the dark, in a twilight, with imperfect vision, constantly mistaking one object for another, imagining distant obstacles where none exists, and unaware of some fatal menace close at hand. This is Frederick Scott Oliver's *Endless Adventure*.

When a party committed to an unalterable doctrine finds itself in a position of power, two things may happen. Leaders who have learnt from experience will exercise their ingenuity in discovering reasons for postponing the part of their programme that they see to be impracticable, or in proving that what appears to be a change is a logical development: in the East, I believe, it is assumed that Marx would have approved, and Lenin acted upon, whatever is done—until the contrary policy is officially adopted. The alternative to such suppleness is the Jacobinism of the obstinate doctrinaire, ready to ruin all rather than modify theory in the face of fact.

Whereas the point of view I have just mentioned, is subject to the alternative dangers of inadaptability, or of adaptation by subterfuge, having committed itself to tenets which it cannot renounce, the danger of the other point of view is equally great: that is the danger of becoming so protean, so endlessly and obligingly adaptable to changing circumstances, that it discredits itself by its indifference to principle. To know what to surrender, and what to hold firm, and indeed to recognize the situation of critical choice when it arises, is an art requiring such resources of experience, wisdom and insight, that I cannot envy those public men, of whatever party, who may at any moment be called upon to make grave decisions, and who may in due course be censured by posterity, either as fanatics or as opportunists. And just as politics of the one type has need constantly to review its tenets and accepted ideas in the light of experience, for otherwise it is in danger of acting on principles that have been discredited, so the politics of the other type needs from time to time to re-open the inquiry as to what are its permanent principles, and review its actions in the light of these principles. For the permanent and the transitory have to be distinguished afresh by each generation.

In an article which I read recently, on the subject of Conservatism in America, the author made the point, which struck me forcibly, that the true conservatives in that country in recent times had none of them been political figures: they had been the philosophic observers and moralists, often in academic positions; and the names he cited were nearly all of men I had known, or with whose work I was acquainted; such men as Paul More and Irving Babbitt in the last generation, and amongst those living, Canon B. I. Bell, and Professor Nisbet of California. If the writer, himself an American, is right, this is not a very healthy state of affairs, unless the views of such writers become more widely diffused and translated, modified, adapted, even adulterated, into action. It seems to me that in a healthy society, there will be a gradation of types between thought and action; at one extreme the detached contemplative, the critical mind which is concerned with the discovery of truth, not with its promulgation and still less with its translation into action, and at the other extreme, the N.C.O. of politics, the man who in spite of relative indifference to general ideas, is equipped with native good sense, right feeling and character, supported by discipline and education. Between these two extremes there is room for several varieties and several kinds of political thinking; but there should be no breach of continuity between them.

At the same time, it is as well that everyone who thinks about politics at all, should recognize his own abilities and limitations, and should not engage in every kind of activity, of those which range from what we call philosophic thought to what we call action. Yet we all understand our own function in society the better for mixing with men of different functions from ours, and the man whose business is merely to think and write, will do his job much better if he has some frequentation of the society of those whose business is to direct policy and make decisions; just as the legislator should be able to put himself at the point of view of those who have to carry out his legislation, and at the point of view of those who have to endure it. There are obviously dangers for society when functions are so sharply divided that men of one profession can no longer understand the mind and temperament of men of another. And to go more directly to the point, a political tradition in which the doctrinaire dominates the man of action, and a tradition in which political philosophy is formulated or re-codified to suit the requirements and justify the conduct of a ruling clique, may be equally disastrous.

I have been making the point that there should be no complete separation of function between men of thought and men of action, and I have maintained that men of different activities, or of political interests, in whom the proportions of the speculative or theoretic and the active were differently mixed, should be able to understand and learn from each other. I have also suggested that it is here, as generally in life, everyone's concern to find out what he ought to meddle with and what he ought to leave alone.

On this last point, I think of a man whom I held in respect and admiration, although some of his views were exasperating and some deplorable—but a great writer, a genuine lover of his country, and a man who deserved a better fate than that which he had in the end to meet. I know that it is easy to criticize a man for not being another man than the man he was; and we should be particularly reserved in criticism of a man whose political setting was that of another country from our own. But with the reservations compelled by this awareness, I have sometimes thought that if Charles Maurras had confined himself to literature, and to the literature of political theory, and had never attempted to found a political party, a *movement*—engaging in, and increasing the acrimony of the political struggle—if he had not given his support to the restoration of the Monarchy in such a way as to strengthen instead of reducing animosities—then those of his ideas which were sound and strong might have spread more widely, and penetrated more deeply, and affected more sensibly the contemporary mind.

But how, in the end, does the work of a mere writer affect political life? One is sometimes tempted to answer that the profounder and *wiser* the man, the less likely is his influence to be discernible. This, of course, is to take a very short view; and at the other extreme, in considering the thought of the very greatest, we can hardly speak of their 'influence' at all: it becomes ridiculous to ask whether the influence of Plato or Aristotle has been good or bad, for we cannot conceive what the history of the European mind would have been without them. Yet the immediate influence of—shall we say—Mr. Bernard Shaw in the period of his most potent influence, I suppose, at the beginning of this century, must have been more appreciable, and more widely diffused, than that of much finer minds: and one is compelled to admire a man of such verbal agility as not only to conceal from his readers and audiences the shallowness of his own thought, but to persuade them that in admiring his work they were giving evidence of their own intelligence as well. I do not say that Shaw could have succeeded alone, without the more plodding and laborious minds with which he associated himself; but by persuading low-brows that they were high-brows, and that high-brows must be socialists, he contributed greatly to the prestige of socialism. But between the influence of a Bernard Shaw or an H. G. Wells, and the influence of a Coleridge or a Newman, I can conceive no common scale of measurement.

I confess, however, that I am not myself very much concerned with the question of influence, or with those publicists who have impressed their names upon the public by catching the morning tide, and rowing very fast in the direction in which the current was flowing; but rather that there should always be a few writers preoccupied in penetrating to the core of the matter, in trying to arrive at the truth and to set it forth, without too much hope, without ambition to alter the immediate course of affairs, and without being downcast or defeated when nothing appears to ensue.

The proper area for such men is what may be called, not the political, but the *pre-political* area. I borrow the term from Canon Demant, the Regius Professor of Theology at Oxford; and I am thinking of work such as his, and Mr. Christopher Dawson's, and that of Professor Reinhold Niebuhr in America. It is in this area also that my own much slighter talents have been employed. But we can look still further for literary influence, not only philosophical, but imaginative, upon politics. Disraeli gained much from his early association with Smythe and Manners, who owed a good deal to Walter Scott. And my defence of the importance of the *pre-political* is simply this, that it is the stratum down to which any sound political thinking must push its roots, and from which it must derive its nourishment. It is also, if you don't mind my changing the metaphor so abruptly, the land in which dwell the Gods of the Copy Book Headings; and, abandoning figurative language altogether, it is the domain of ethics—in the end, the domain of theology. For the question of questions, which no political philosophy can escape, and by the right answer to which all political thinking must in the end be judged, is simply this: What is Man? what are his limitations? what is his misery and what his greatness? and what, finally, his destiny?

THE CLASSICS AND THE MAN OF LETTERS[1]

Not very long ago, an eminent author, in the course of expressing his views about the future of education after this war, went a little out of his way to declare that in the new order there would still be a place for Greek. He qualified this concession, however, by explaining that the study of Greek was a field of scholarship of equal dignity with Egyptology, and several other specialized studies which he named, and that the opportunity to pursue these studies should, in any liberal society, be provided for the few who were particularly drawn to them. I read this in one of the periodicals which are found in the waiting-rooms of certain experts in applied science; and having neglected to make a note of the passage before being summoned to my professional appointment, I cannot quote chapter and verse, and therefore withhold the name of the author. But this statement, made without irony and wholly in a spirit of enlightened generosity, started the train of thought which I propose to continue here. I am grateful to the writer for having suggested to my mind the only possible role in which I can present myself on this occasion. In my earlier years I obtained, partly by subtlety, partly by effrontery, and partly by accident, a reputation amongst the credulous for learning and scholarship, of which (having no further use for it) I have since tried to disembarrass myself. Better to confess one's weaknesses, when they are certain to be revealed sooner or later, than to leave them to be exposed by posterity: though it is, I have discovered, easier in our times to acquire an undeserved reputation for learning than to get rid of it: but that is neither here nor there. My point is that if I made those claims for the classics which

[1] The Presidential Address to the Classical Association at Cambridge on April 15th, 1942.

can only be supported by the erudition of the scholar, or those which can only be pleaded by what we now call the education*ist*, I might jeopardize the cause: for there are far better scholars than I, who attach less importance to the study of Latin and Greek than I do, and there are teachers who can demonstrate the impracticability of the studies which I should like to promote. But if I present the defence of the classics merely from the point of view of the man of letters, I am on safer ground: and I think you will agree that the claim to be a man of letters is, after all, a modest pretension. I must, however, begin by explaining why I have used this rather indefinite term, and what I mean by it.

If I were more specific, and spoke of 'the poet', 'the novelist', 'the dramatist', or 'the critic', I should suggest to your minds a number of particular considerations which would distract your attention from the view of literature as a whole which I wish to keep before us in the present context. Take, for instance, the term 'poet' and the objections which it would immediately evoke. We are commonly inclined to assume that the creation of literature, and poetry especially, depends simply upon the unpredictable appearance from time to time of writers of genius; that genius cannot be brought into the world at will, and that when it does appear it is likely to break every rule, that no system of education can foster it, and no system of education can stifle it. If we look at literature as merely a succession of great writers, instead of looking at the literature of one European language as something which forms a significant whole in itself, and a significant part in the literature of Europe, this is the view we are likely to take. Taking this view, we look at each great writer by himself; and looking at him by himself, we are unlikely to believe that he would have been a greater writer, or an inferior writer, if he had had a different kind of education. The defects of a great writer's background are inextricably confused with its advantages; just as the shortcomings of his character are indissolubly associated with his shining virtues, and his material difficulties with his success. Can we regret, for instance, that François Villon did not choose to mix with more respectable society, or that Robert Burns did not have the same schooling as Dr. Johnson? The life of a man of genius, viewed in relation to his writing, comes to take a pattern of inevitability, and even his disabilities will seem to have stood him in good stead.

This way of looking at a great poet or novelist or dramatist, is half of the truth: it is what we find when we look at one writer after another, without balancing this point of view by the imaginative grasp of a national literature as a whole. I wanted to make it clear that I do not pretend that a classical education is essential for the writer of genius: and unless I can suggest to your minds that a great literature is more than the sum of a number of great writers, that it has a character of its own, much of my contention will be misunderstood. It is because I do not want to concentrate your attention upon the man of genius that I have used the term 'man of letters'. This includes men of the second or third, or lower ranks as well as the greatest; and these secondary writers provide collectively, and individually in varying degrees, an important part of the environment of the great writer, as well as his first audience, his first appreciators, his first critical correctors—and perhaps his first detractors. The continuity of a literature is essential to its greatness; it is very largely the function of secondary writers to preserve this continuity, and to provide a body of writings which is not necessarily read by posterity, but which plays a great part in forming the link between those writers who continue to be read. This continuity is largely unconscious, and only visible in historical retrospect: I need only refer you for evidence to the monumental, though brief, essay by Professor R. W. Chambers on *The Continuity of English Prose*. And it is within this continuity, and within this environment, that, for my present purpose, individual authors have to be considered. When we look at them in this way, we can see that, among the great, even some of the most formal and correct have been also innovators and even rebels, and that even some of the most revolutionary have carried on the work of those from whose influence they rebelled.

It would be easy, indeed, to muster an army of great names, of men who have become great writers with very little educational advantage. Bunyan and Abraham Lincoln are only two among the names more frequently cited. These men, and others, learned how to use the English language very largely from the English Bible: and it is the tritest commonplace that a knowledge of the Bible, Shakespeare, and Bunyan (I might add the Book of Common Prayer) could teach a man of genius, or a man of first-rate ability short of genius, all that he needs in order to write English well. But I would remark first, that it is by no means irrelevant that the translators of that English Bible were great scholars in their time as well as great stylists; and we have to ask, not merely what had Shakespeare and Bunyan read, but what had the English authors read whose works nourished Shakespeare and Bunyan? And I would remark next, that the education given to Shakespeare, or Bunyan, or Lincoln, would be about the most difficult kind to get today. It would be much more reasonable to expect to find a poet with the learning of a Ben Jonson or a Milton than either a poet or prose writer who had had the advantages of Shakespeare or Bunyan. No schoolmaster could afford the reputation of sending his pupils forth as ill-furnished as these men were. And there is too much to read for anybody to be expected to master, and to believe in, a few authors; apart from the fact that out of school there is every pressure to write badly, to talk incoherently, and to think confusedly.

It should be apparent at this point, that our primary concern in considering the education of the man of letters, is not the amount of learning which a man acquires, the number of years during which he is subjected to the educational process, or the degree of scholastic distinction which he attains: what is of prime importance is the type of education within which his schooling falls. The most instructive contrast of degree of education within the same type is that provided by Shakespeare and Milton, our two greatest poets. We can say of Shakespeare, that never has a man turned so little knowledge to such great account: we must couple Milton with Dante, in saying that never has a poet possessed of such great learning so completely justified the acquisition of it. Shakespeare's education, what he had of it, belongs in the same tradition as that of Milton: it was essentially a classical education. The significance of a type of education may lie almost as much in what it omits as in what it includes. Shakespeare's classical knowledge appears to have been derived largely from translations. But he lived in a world in which the wisdom of the ancients was respected, and their poetry admired and enjoyed; he was less well educated than many of his colleagues, but this was education of the same kind–and it is almost more important, for a man of letters, that his associates should be well educated than that he should be well educated himself. The standards and the values were there; and Shakespeare himself had that ability, which is not native to everyone, to extract the utmost possible from translations. In these two advantages he had what mattered most.

If Shakespeare's knowledge was fragmentary and second-hand, that of Milton was comprehensive and direct. A lesser poet, with the learning and tastes of Milton, would have been in danger of becoming a mere pedant in verse. An understanding of Milton's poetry requires some acquaintance with several subjects none of which are very much in favour today; a knowledge of the Bible, not necessarily in Hebrew and Greek, but certainly in English; a knowledge of classical literature, mythology and history of Latin syntax and versification and of Christian theology. Some knowledge of Latin is necessary, not only for understanding what Milton is talking about, but much more for understanding his style and his music. It is not that Milton's vocabulary is excessively weighted with Latin words: there was more of that in the previous century. An acquaintance with Latin is necessary if we are to understand, and to accept, the involutions of his sentence structure, and if we are to hear the complete music of his verse. The present generation may miss, what we cannot expect from Milton, the colloquial style, the sound of the conversational voice, the range of mood and emotion which requires a more homely diction for its expression; it may sometimes find his syntax tortured. Milton has been reproached, and there is some truth behind the reproach, for writing English like a dead language: I think it was Landor who said so, and Landor is a critic to be treated with respect. Milton's was certainly a style fatal to imitators: that is just as true of the style of James Joyce, and the influence of a great writer upon other writers can neither add to nor detract from his title to honour. The point is that Milton's Latinism is essential to his greatness, and that I have only chosen him as the extreme example of English poetry in general. You may write English poetry without knowing any Latin; I am not so sure whether without Latin you can wholly understand it. I believe, and have said elsewhere, that the rich possibilities of English verse—possibilities still unexhausted—owe much to the variety of racial strains bringing in a variety of speech and verse rhythms; and that English verse also owes much to the fact that Greek for three hundred years, and Latin for longer than that, have gone to its formation. And what I have said of verse can be applied to prose also, though perhaps with less compulsion: can we really enter into the style of Clarendon unless we have at least a smattering of Tacitus, or the style of Gibbon unless we have some awareness of the immense power upon him of the classical and post-classical chroniclers, the patristic and post-patristic theologians, who provided him with his material?

If a classical education is the background for English literature in the past, we are justified in affirming not merely that a good knowledge of Latin (if not of Greek) should be expected of those who teach English literature, but that some knowledge of Latin should be expected of those who study it. This is not quite the direction, however, which I propose to pursue. I am not here concerned with the teaching of literature, but with teaching only in relation to those who are going to write it. For many generations the classics provided the basis of the education of the people from whom the majority of our men of letters have sprung: which is far from saying that the majority of our men of letters have been recruited from any limited social class. This common basis of education has, I believe, had a great part in giving English letters of the past that unity which gives us the right to say that we have not only produced a succession of great writers, but a literature, and a literature which is a distinguished part of a recognizable entity called Europe Literature. We are then justified in inquiring what is likely to happen, to our language and our literature, when the connection between the classics and our own literature is completely broken, when the classical scholar is as completely specialized as the Egyptologist, and when the poet or the critic whose mind and taste have been exercised on Latin and Greek literature will be more exceptional than the dramatist who has prepared himself for his task in the theatre by a close study of optical, electrical, and acoustical physics? You have the option of welcoming the change as the dawn of emancipation, or of deploring it as the twilight of literature; but at least you must agree that we might expect it to mark some great difference between the literature of the past and that of the future—perhaps so great as to be the transition from an old language to a new one.

In the past twenty years I have observed what seems to me a deterioration in the middle literary stratum, and notably in the standards and the scholarship which are wanted for literary criticism. Lest you judge too hastily that this complaint is merely the creak of rheumatic middle age, I will quote a representative of a younger literary generation than my own, Mr. Michael Roberts:

'By the summer of 1939 there were only two serious literary papers in England: an admirable quarterly called *Scrutiny*, with a small circulation, and the *Times Literary Supplement*, which like the more serious libraries, had fewer readers in 1938 than in 1922. The notion of quality became submerged in the idea that "it's all a matter of taste", and the untutored taste of the individual was tempered only by the fear of being excessively eccentric or excessively conventional. One ingenious publisher succeeded in making the best of both worlds by advertising "A Novel for a Few People. 20th Thousand."'

The reasons for such a decline are no doubt complex, and I am not going to suggest that this is all due to the neglect of classical studies, or that a revival of these studies would be enough to stem the current. But the disappearance of any common background of instruction, any common body of literary and historical knowledge, any common acquaintance with the foundations of English literature, has probably made it easier for writers to comply with the pressure of tendencies for which they were not responsible. One function of criticism–I am not thinking of the great critics or the classics of criticism, but rather of the hebdomadary reviewer, formerly anonymous, who has now more often the publicity of signature, though seldom the satisfaction of higher pay–one function of criticism is to act as a kind of cog regulating the rate of change of literary taste. When the cog sticks, and reviewers remain fast in the taste of a previous generation, the machine needs to be ruthlessly dismantled and reassembled; when it slips, and the reviewer accepts novelty as a sufficient criterion of excellence, the machine needs to be stopped and tightened up. The effect of either fault in the machine is to cause a division between those who see no good in anything that is new, and those who see no good in anything else: the antiquation of the old, and the eccentricity and even charlatanism of the new, are both thereby accelerated. The effect of this failure of criticism is to place the serious writer in a dilemma: either to write for too large a public or to write for too small a public. And the curious result of either choice, is to place a premium on the ephemeral. The novelty of a work of imagination which is only popular, and has nothing really new in it, soon wears off: for a later generation will prefer the original to the copy, when both belong to the past. And the novelty of anything that is merely new produces only a momentary shock: the same work will not produce the same shock twice, but must be followed by something newer.

The charge has been brought against the more original literature of our time, that it has been written for a small and exclusive audience–an audience not small and exclusive because it was the best, but because (so it has been alleged) it consisted of perverse, eccentric, or anti-social people with their snobbish parasites. This appears to be an accusation which the most dissimilar groups can concur in bringing: the conservative who regard anything new as anarchic, and the radical who regard anything they do not understand as undemocratic. With the political passions enlisted for the support of these judgments, I am not here concerned. My point is that this is a consequence, not of individual aberrancy–though it creates a situation in which the sham can easily pass, for a time and with some readers, as genuine—but of social disintegration: in the literary aspect, of critical decay. It arises from the lack of continuous communication, of the artist with his friends and fellow artists and the small number of keen amateurs of the arts, with a larger public educated in the same way; of taste cultivated upon the literature of the past but ready to accept what is good in the present when that is brought to their notice, and so with the world at large. If an author's first discriminating readers are themselves isolated from the larger world, their influence upon him may be unbalanced: their taste is in danger of yielding to their group prejudice and fancy, and they may easily succumb to the temptation of overvaluing the achievement of their members and favourite authors.

It is one thing to pass these strictures upon the present condition of literature, or to voice forebodings of its diminished future, and quite another to put forward positive suggestions about the type of education most profitable for the man of letters, and the way in which it could be fitted into the general educational scheme. In concern with education we are attentive to the problems of the child and the adolescent; very largely to the average or the mediocre child; very largely to the child whose educational opportunities have heretofore been meagre. When we think of the larger pattern we are apt to think (quite rightly) in terms of the production of good citizens. The question I leave with you is the question whether we think the maintenance of the greatness of our literature a matter of sufficient importance to be taken account of, in our educational planning, at all? and even if we agree about its importance, whether education can take any responsibility for it? The answer may be, No. But the question must be asked, and the answer must not be a hasty answer. The right answer can only come after some very hard thinking, and thinking with very wide scope, by many people. I would not dissimulate the difficulty. The problem of training an adequate supply of good scientists, in various departments, is one very much with us; it is, I imagine, one much more readily capable of solution than is my problem. But I do not think that it would seem so much more soluble, were it not that we all recognize, under the pressure of material evidence, its necessity; and I think that agreement on the importance of a problem makes the solution of it much more likely.

I can see that the proper training of a man with the scientific bent, even now when the ramifications of the sciences are so extensive and the knowledge to be assimilated in any branch of science so vast, is more readily susceptible of precise determination. So, for that matter, is the training for any other art than that of letters. The painter, the sculptor, the architect, the musician, though they may have more difficulty in scraping a living, or in combining the pursuit of their art with an unrelated stipendiary job, all have a much more definite technique to master than that of the writer. Their essential training is more technical; the subjects which they must learn are more clearly indicated; and they do not need that varied general culture without which the man of letters is ill-equipped. Another difference, not unconnected with the foregoing, is that literary ability does not, with any certainty, manifest itself so early, or with such precise confidence of its goal, as does a bent towards another art. A desire to express oneself in verse is (or so my experience inclines me to believe) a trait of the majority of Anglo-Saxons of both sexes at some stage of their development: it may persist long after the lack of vocation is patent to everyone except the authors themselves. When a schoolboy composes good verses, we are justified in expecting that he will, in later life, excel in some pursuit or other—but that pursuit may take him very far from poetry or letters—it may lead toward the bar or the episcopal bench. The truly literary mind is likely to develop slowly; it needs a more comprehensive and more varied diet, a more miscellaneous knowledge of facts, a greater experience of men and of ideas, than the kind required for the practice of the other arts. It therefore presents a more baffling educational problem. In saying this, I am not arrogating any preeminence for that art of letters itself: I am merely pointing out a difference in the preparation.

I should like to make clear at this point that there are several arguments in favour of the classical education with which, however cogent and sufficient, I am not here concerned. Into the question whether all children, whatever their destination, should be taught elementary Latin, and perhaps Greek–the question whether it is desirable, and then whether it is practicable–I shall not venture. I would only remark that the question of the age up to which all children should have the same education, and the question of the common element in all education up to a later stage, is a very important one even from the point of view of the man of letters: for upon this depends the possibility of a general audience, the possibility both of the author's being able to communicate with people in all walks of life, and of their being able to understand each other. I would also observe in passing, that to postpone the introduction to Latin to the age at which a boy appears to be more gifted for languages than for other studies is to postpone it too long–apart from my belief that it would be most desirable for everyone to possess some knowledge of Latin even if none of Greek. I am not here interested, however, in the advocacy of the study of these two languages as 'mental discipline'. I think that the defence of any study purely as 'discipline' in the modern sense can be maintained too obstinately: I have, for instance, heard compulsory chapel defended, by an unbeliever, on the ground that it was good for boys to have a duty which they disliked so much. The defence of 'discipline' in the abstract, the belief that any 'mental discipline' carried out in the right way and far enough will produce an abstract 'educated man', seems to have some relation to the egalitarian tendencies of the nineteenth century which extended to subjects of study the same ideal of equality held for the human beings who might study them. A *disciple*, at any rate, is surely a willing pupil, and one who attaches himself to a master voluntarily, because he believes in the value of the subject which the master professes and believes that that master is qualified to give him the initiation he wants. Discipleship, that is, starts by a valuation–by the desire to attain to some particular knowledge or proficiency, not by the desire for training in the abstract followed by the judgment that this subject of study will provide it. For my purpose it is the value of the subject that is in question, not the incidental and necessary 'discipline' by which its command is attained. And as I am not considering discipline in the abstract, so I am not considering 'education' in the abstract, or the somewhat barren question of the definition of the abstract 'educated man'.

For my purposes, also, the distinction between 'vocational'and 'cultural' education is of little use: apart from the disadvantage that 'vocational' is apt to connote merely a salary and a pension, and 'cultural' to connote an 'education for leisure' which is either a refined hedonism or a skill to practise harmless hobbies. The writer, *qua* writer, seldom draws a salary, and he has no problem of occupying a supposed leisure. Everything may be grist to his mill, and the more knowledge of every kind that he can assimilate the better: the serious distinction, for him, is between the subjects which he should be taught, and the subjects which he should acquire by himself. His business is communication through language: when he is an imaginative writer, he is engaged in the most difficult form of communication, where precision is of the utmost importance, a precision which cannot be given beforehand but has to be found in every new phrase. In order to understand language in the way in which the man of letters should understand it, we must know the various purposes for which language has been used; and that involves some knowledge of the subjects for the communication of which men have used language in the past: notably of history, for you cannot understand the literature of the past without some knowledge of the conditions under which it was written, and the sort of people who wrote it; of logic, for that is an investigation of the anatomy of thought in language; of philosophy, for that is the attempt to use language in the most abstract way possible.

Into this already formidable programme we have to introduce at some stage at least one modern foreign language as well as our own language and classics. It should be a major language with a parallel development to our own, and with a flourishing contemporary literature; for we are greatly helped to develop objectivity of taste if we can appreciate the work of foreign authors; living in the same world as ourselves, and expressing thier vision of it in another great language. The possession of several foreign languages is of course better than of one alone; but it is impossible to understand the language, the literature, and the people of more than one foreign country equally well. In our time, the most important foreign language for the man of letters, has been French: and I need not remind you that for French a knowledge of Latin is still more important, and a knowledge of Greek hardly less important, than for English. For a man of very exceptional linguistic ability, who was not already sunk beneath the burden of the acquirements I recommend, I believe that an acquaintance with some great and more remote language might be a very valuable addition; Hebrew suggests itself, but both for extreme difference of structure and intellectual dignity a very good choice would be Chinese: but to mention this is to scan the very horizon of possibility.

All these branches of learning have to be acquired through teachers; and there does not appear to be much space left in the curriculum for scientific subjects. I am assuming however that my excellent man of letters will have had (what I did not attain) enough training at school in the language of mathematics not to be completely baffled when he attempts, by himself, to understand the general significance of some scientific discovery. The only reason of universal applicability, why he could not acquire more detailed scientific knowledge in his formal education, is the very obvious one that there was not time: for I have allowed for some hours to be spent in eating, sleeping, social ritual, conviviality, worship, athletic activities, and physical training. It is most desirable that he should be able, throughout his life, to take an interest in subjects in which he has not been trained; for, as I have suggested, to a person of some power of imagination almost anything can be of use. It is sometimes suggested that the wonders of science provide nourishment for the imagination. I am sure they can; but I think a distinction should be drawn between the imagination of a great scientist, arriving at a discovery on the basis of observed phenomena, the significance of which has escaped other equally well trained and informed scientists, and the imagination of a Lucretius, or even a Shelley, informing their scientific knowledge with an emotional life with which the scientist, as such, has no concern.

I have not, as you see, been urging the claims of 'cultural' or general, education against specialized; for in its way, the education of the man of letters must be itself specialized and 'vocational'. But we have to face one more difficulty. I have made clear that I am not attempting to legislate for the man of genius, but for the environment of men of letters into which he will be born or find his way. But on the other hand you cannot draw a sharp line between the man of letters and his audience, between the critic in print and the critic in conversation. Nobody suffers more from being limited to the society of his own profession than does the writer: it is still worse when his audience is composed chiefly of other writers or would-be writers. He needs a small public of substantially the same education as himself, as well as the same tastes; a larger public with some common background with him; and finally he should have something in common with everyone who has intelligence and sensibility and can read his language. The problem of the survival of English literature, therefore, brings us to the problem of the need for unity in education, the need for some unification which will not be to the detriment of any of the branches of learning and investigation, scientific or humanistic. This problem, so much greater than any problem of administration, organization, or curricular devices, because it is a spiritual problem, because its solution involves not merely planning, but *growing* a pattern of values, is so vast a problem that it is not one for the educational specialist alone, but for all who are concerned with the structure of society. It is one with which I have no more to do here than to show my awareness of it. My only contribution is to proclaim that the future of English Literature will be deeply affected by the way in which we solve or fail to solve this problem.

My particular thesis has been that the maintenance of classical education is essential to the maintenance of the continuity of English Literature. How, and by what adaptation to the necessary, the desirable, and the inevitable, the place for the classics in education is to be found is not a subject on which I have the right to claim your attention. But I am sure that this is one important line of defence of the classics. The standards of the highest scholarship have to be kept up, and the work of research honoured:

it is necessary that the prestige of the great scholars should not be allowed to dwindle. That there will continue to be a place for the great scholar—without whom the whole fabric of classical education crumbles—I do not doubt: what is less certain is that in the future he will be discovered young enough to be given the proper training; and that he will be allowed any greater role than that of preparing a few younger men to carry on his work, without prospect of wider influence. The second group is that of non-professional scholarship and of scholarship in other fields in which an accurate knowledge of the classical languages is, or should be required; it includes not only the theologians and the historians, but the clergy and ministry, the teachers of modern language and literature, and the literary critics. For the last of these, certainly, it should hardly be enough that he should have spent some years at school in acquiring the languages, if he never afterwards opens a text: he must have the literature accessible and operative in his taste and judgment; he must be able to enjoy it. But the maintenance of these types of scholarship is not enough or even possible unless some knowledge of the civilizations of Greece and Rome, some respect for their achievements, some understanding of their historical relation to our own, and some acquaintance with their literature and their wisdom *in translation* can be cultivated among a very much larger number of people: among those who (like myself) have not remembered enough to read the originals with ease, and among those who have never studied the languages at all. A limited preserve of scholarship will be ineffectual unless a much wider respect for, and appreciation of the relevance of, the subject-matter of this scholarship can be disseminated amongst those who will never be given the first-hand knowledge.

My assertions about the dependence of English Literature upon the Latin and Greek literatures, will, I am aware, have no persuasive influence whatever upon several classes of people. There are those who do not believe that literature is a matter of any great importance, and those who, while conceding a certain value to the literature of the past, do not consider it of great importance that English Literature should continue to take a front rank. There are those who acknowledge the importance of literature, but do not believe that one type of education or another will make much difference to its further survival. There are those who, immersed perhaps in the immense difficulties of providing some sort of education or other to the whole of the nation, consider this extra problem less urgent, or complain that they have so many other things to think of that it is more than can be coped with. And finally, there are those who want so new a world that they even welcome the prospect of a breach of continuity. And in many minds, no doubt, all of these attitudes can co-exist in a half-formed state; now one, now another, presenting itself in consciousness.

To attempt to confute all these objections would be an impertinence in the present company, and some of them come much more within the province of those who have had life-long experience of the classroom and the council chamber. My appeal can only address itself to those who already accept the contention that the preservation of a living literature is more than a matter of interest only to amateurs of verse and readers of novels; and who see in it the preservation of developed speech, and of civilization against barbarism. They will be those also who appreciate the need, if the present chaos is ever to be reduced to order, of something more than an administrative or an economic unification—the need of a cultural unification in diversity of Europe; and who believe that a new unity can only grow on the old roots: the Christian Faith, and the classical languages which Europeans inherit in common. These roots are, I think, inextricably intertwined. I should not care to risk the heresy, upon which some religious-political writers have appeared to verge, of regarding Christianity as a European, rather than a universal Faith: I do not wish to be accused of inventing a new heresy to the effect that salvation depends upon getting a first in classics. But the culture of Europe, such as it is, is a Christian culture; and conversely, the traditional religious faith of Europe, including Britain, cannot preserve its intellectual vigour unless a high standard of Latin and Greek scholarship is maintained amongst its teachers. But these considerations are beyond the mandate which I have assumed for this occasion. And I do not wish to leave you with the impression that I am asking too much of formal education, either in the sphere of religion or in that of literature: I am quite aware that an educational system cannot of itself bring about either great faith or great literature: it is truer to say that our education is not so much the generator of our culture as the offspring of it. But those who care for the preservation, the extension, and the advancement of our culture cannot fail to interest themselves, however unqualified they may be to pass judgment, in our classical heritage.

EZRA POUND: HIS METRIC AND POETRY[1]

I

'All talk on modern poetry, by people who know,' wrote Mr. Carl Sandburg in *Poetry*, 'ends with dragging in Ezra Pound somewhere. He may be named only to be cursed as wanton and mocker, poseur, trifler and vagrant. Or he may be classed as filling a niche today like that of Keats in a preceding epoch. The point is, he will be mentioned.'

This is a simple statement of fact. But though Mr. Pound is well known, even having been the victim of interviews for Sunday papers, it does not follow that his work is thoroughly known. There are twenty people who have their opinion of him for every one who has read his writings with any care. Of those twenty, there will be some who are shocked, some who are ruffled, some who are irritated, and one or two whose sense of dignity is outraged. The twenty-first critic will probably be one who knows and admires some of the poems, but who either says: 'Pound is primarily a scholar, a translator,' or 'Pound's early verse was beautiful; his later work shows nothing better than the itch for advertisement, a mischievous desire to be annoying, or a childish desire to be original.' There is a third type of reader, rare enough, who has perceived Mr. Pound for some years, who has followed his career intelligently, and who recognizes its consistency.

This essay is not written for the first twenty critics of literature, nor for that rare twenty-second who has just been mentioned, but for the admirer of a poem here or there, whose appreciation

[1] This little book was issued anonymously on November 12th, 1917 (New York, Alfred A. Knopf).

is capable of yielding him a larger return. If the reader is already at the stage where he can maintain at once the two propositions, 'Pound is merely a scholar' and 'Pound is merely a yellow journalist,' or the other two propositions, 'Pound is merely a technician' and 'Pound is merely a prophet of chaos,' then there is very little hope. But there are readers of poetry who have not yet reached this hypertrophy of the logical faculty; their attention might yet be arrested, not by an outburst of praise, but by a simple statement. The present essay aims merely at such a statement. It is not intended to be either a biographical or a critical study. It will not dilate upon 'beauties'; it is a summary account of ten years' work in poetry. The citations from reviews will perhaps stimulate the reader to form his own opinion. We do not wish to form it for him. Nor shall we enter into other phases of Mr. Pound's activity during this ten years; his writings and view on art and music; though these would take an important place in any comprehensive biography.

II

Pound's first book was published in Venice. Venice was a halting point after he had left America and before he had settled in England, and here, in 1908, *A Lume Spento* appeared. The volume is now a rarity of literature; it was published by the author and made at a Venetian press where the author was able personally to supervise the printing; on paper which was a remainder of a supply which has been used for a History of the Church. Pound left Venice in the same year, and took *A Lume Spento* with him to London. It was not to be expected that a first book of verse, published by an unknown American in Venice, should attract much attention. *The Evening Standard* has the distinction of having noticed the volume, in a review summing it up as:

'wild and haunting stuff, absolutely poetic, original, imaginative, passionate, and spiritual. Those who do not consider it crazy may well consider it inspired. Coming after the trite and decorous verse of most of our decorous poets, this poet seems like a minstrel of Provence at a suburban musical evening . . . The unseizable magic of poetry is in the queer paper volume, and words are no good in describing it.'

As the chief poems in *A Lume Spento* were afterwards incorporated in *Personae*, the book demands mention only as a date in the author's history. *Personae*, the first book published in London, followed early in 1909. Few poets have undertaken the siege of London with so little backing; few books of verse have ever owed their success so purely to their own merits. Pound came to London a complete stranger, without either literary patronage or financial means. He took *Personae* to Mr. Elkin Mathews, who has the glory of having published Yeats' *Wind Among the Reeds*, and the *Book of the Rhymers' Club*, in which many of the poets of the '90s, now famous, found a place. Mr. Mathews first suggested, as was natural to an unknown author, that the author should bear part of the cost of printing. 'I have a shilling in my pocket, if that is any use to you,' said the latter. 'Well,' said Mr. Mathews, 'I want to publish it anyway.' His acumen was justified. The book was, it is true, received with opposition, but it was received. There were a few appreciative critics, notably Mr. Edward Thomas, the poet (known also as 'Edward Eastaway'; he has since been killed in France). Thomas, writing in the *English Review* (then in its brightest days under the editorship of Ford Madox Hueffer), recognized the first-hand intensity of feeling in *Personae*:

'He has . . . hardly any of the superficial good qualities of modern versifiers . . . He has not the current melancholy or resignation or unwillingness to live; nor the kind of feeling for nature which runs to minute description and decorative metaphor. He cannot be usefully compared with any living writers; . . . full of personality and with such power to express it, that from the first to the last lines of most of his poems he holds us steadily in his own pure grave, passionate world . . . The beauty of it "In Praise of Ysolt" is the beauty of passion, sincerity and intensity, not of beautiful words and images and suggestions . . . the thought dominates the words and is greater than they are. Here "Idyll for Glaucus" the effect is full of human passion and natural magic, without any of the phrases which a reader of modern verse would expect in the treatment of such a subject.'

Mr. Scott James, in the *Daily News*, speaks in praise of his metres:

'At first the whole thing may seem to be mere madness and rhetoric, a vain exhibition of force and passion without beauty. But, as we read on, these curious metres of his seem to have a law and order of their own; the brute force of Mr. Pound's imagination seems to impart some quality of infectious beauty to his words. Sometimes there is a strange beating of anapaests when he quickens to his subject; again and again he unexpectedly ends a line with the second half of a reverberant hexameter:

Flesh shrouded, bearing the secret.

. . . and a few lines later comes an example of his favourite use of spondee, followed by dactyl and spondee, which comes in strangely and, as we first read it, with the appearance of discord, but afterwards seems to gain a curious and distinctive vigour:

Eyes, dreams, lips, and the night goes.

Another line like the end of a hexameter is:

But if e'er I come to my love's land.

But even so favourable a critic pauses to remark that:

'He baffles us by archaic words and unfamiliar metres; he often seems to be scorning the limitations of form and metre, breaking out into any sort of expression which suits itself to his mood.'

and counsels the poet to 'have a little more respect for his art'.

It is, in fact, just this adaptability of metre to mood, an adaptability due to an intensive study of metre, that constitutes an important element in Pound's technique. Few readers were prepared to accept or follow the amount of erudition which entered into *Personae* and its close successor, *Exultations*, or to devote the care to reading them which they demand. It is here that many have been led astray. Pound is not one of those poets who make no demands of the reader; and the casual reader of verse, disconcerted by the difference between Pound's poetry and that on which his taste has been trained, attributes his own difficulties to excessive scholarship on the part of the author. 'This', he will say of some of the poems in Provençal form or on Provençal subjects, 'is archaeology; it requires knowledge on the part of its reader, and true poetry does not require such knowledge.' But to display knowledge is not the same thing as to expect it on the part of the reader; and of this sort of pedantry Pound is quite free. He is, it is true, one of the most learned of poets. In America he had taken up the study of Romance Languages with the intention of teaching. After work in Spain and Italy, after pursuing the Provençal verb from Milan to Freiburg, he deserted the thesis on Lope de Vega and the Ph.D. and the professorial chair, and elected to remain in Europe. Mr. Pound has spoken out his mind from time to time on the subject of scholarship in American universities, its deadness, its isolation from genuine appreciation, and the active creative life of literature. He has always been ready to battle against pedantry. As for his own learning, he has studied poetry carefully, and has made use of his study in his own verse. *Personae* and *Exultations* show his talent for turning his studies to account. He was supersaturated in Provence; he had tramped over most of the country; and the life of the courts where the Troubadours thronged was part of his own life to him. Yet, though *Personae* and *Exultations* do exact something from the reader, they do not require a knowledge of Provençal or of Spanish or Italian. Very few people know the Arthurian legends well, or even Malory (if they did they might realize that the *Idylls of the King* are hardly more important than a parody, or a 'Chaucer retold for Children'); but no one accuses Tennyson of needing footnotes, or of superciliousness toward the uninstructed. The difference is merely in what people are prepared for; most readers could no more relate the myth of Atys correctly than they could give a biography of Bertrand de Born. It is hardly too much to say that there is no poem in these volumes of Mr. Pound which needs fuller explanation than he gives himself. What the poems do require is a trained ear, or at least the willingness to be trained.

The metres and the use of language are unfamiliar. There are certain traces of modern influence. We cannot agree with Mr. Scott James that among these are 'W. E. Henley, Kipling, Chatterton, and especially Walt Whitman'—least of all Walt Whitman. Probably there are only two: Yeats and Browning. Yeats in 'La Fraisne', in *Personae*, for instance, in the attitude and somewhat in the vocabulary:

I wrapped my tears in an ellum leaf
And left them under a stone,
And now men call me mad because I have thrown
All folly from me, putting it aside
To leave the old barren ways of men . . .

For Browning, Mr. Pound has always professed strong admiration (see 'Mesmerism' in *Personae*); there are traces of him in 'Cino' and 'Famam Librosque Cano', in the same volume. But it is more profitable to comment upon the variety of metres and the original use of language.

Ezra Pound has been fathered with vers libre in English, with all its vices and virtues. The term is a loose one—any verse is called 'free' by people whose ears are not accustomed to it—in the second place, Pound's use of this medium has shown the temperance of the artist, and his belief in it as a vehicle is not that of the fanatic. He has said himself that when one has the proper material for a sonnet, one should use the sonnet form; but that it happens very rarely to any poet to find himself in possession of just the block of stuff which can perfectly be modelled into the sonnet. It is true that up to very recently it was impossible to get free verse printed in any periodical except those in which Pound had influence; and that now it is possible to print free verse (second, third or tenth-rate) in almost any American magazine. Who is responsible for the bad free verse is a question of no importance, inasmuch as its authors would have written bad verse in any form; Pound has at least the right to be judged by the success or failure of his own. Pound's vers libre is such as is only possible for a poet who has worked tirelessly with rigid forms and different systems of metric. His *Canzoni* are in a way aside from his direct line of progress; they are much more nearly studies in mediaeval appreciation than any of his other verse; but they are interesting, apart from their merit, as showing the poet at work with the most intricate Provençal forms—so intricate that the pattern cannot be exhibited without quoting an entire poem. (M. Jean de Bosschère, whose French is translated in the *Egoist*, has already called attention to the fact that Pound was the first writer in English to use five Provençal forms.) Quotation will show, however, the great variety of rhythm which Pound manages to introduce into the ordinary iambic pentameter:

Thy gracious ways,
O lady of my heart, have
O'er all my thought their golden glamour cast;
As amber torch-flames, where strange men-at-arms
Tread softly 'neath the damask shield of night,
Rise from the flowing steel in part reflected,
So on my mailed thought that with thee goeth,
Though dark the way, a golden glamour falleth.

Within the iambic limits, there are no two lines in the whole poem that have an identical rhythm.

We turn from this to a poem in *Exultations*, the 'Night Litany':

O God, what great kindness
have we done in times past
and forgotten it,
That thou givest this wonder unto us,
O God of waters?

O God of the night
What great sorrow
Cometh unto us,
That thou thus repayest us
Before the time of its coming?

There is evident, and more strongly in certain later poems, a tendency toward quantitative measure. Such a 'freedom' as this lays so heavy a burden upon every word in a line that it becomes impossible to write like Shelley, leaving blanks for the adjectives, or like Swinburne, whose adjectives are practically blanks. Other poets have manipulated a great variety of metres and forms; but few have studied the forms and metres which they use so carefully as has Pound. His ballad of the 'Goodly Fere' shows great knowledge of the ballad form:

I ha' seen him cow a thousand men
On the hills o' Galilee,
They whined as he walked out calm between
Wi' his eyes like the grey o' the sea.

Like the sea that brooks no voyaging
With the winds unleashed and free,
Like the sea that he cowed at Genseret
Wi' twey words spoke suddently.

A master of men was the Goodly Fere
A mate of the wind and sea,
If they think they ha' slain our Goodly Fere
They are fools eternally.

I ha' seen him eat o' the honey-comb,
Sin' they nailed him to the tree.

And from this we turn to a very different form in the 'Altaforte', which is perhaps the best sestina that has been written in English:

Damn it all! all this our South stinks peace.
You whoreson dog, Papiols, come! let's to music!
I have no life save when the swords clash.
But ah! when I see the standards gold, vair, purple, opposing,
And the broad fields beneath them turn crimson,
Then howl I my heart nigh mad with rejoicing.

In hot summer have I great rejoicing
When the tempests kill the earth's foul peace,
And the lightnings from black heaven flash crimson,
And the fierce thunders roar me their music
And the winds shriek through the clouds man, opposing,
And through all the riven skies God's swords clash.

I have quoted two verses to show the intricacy of the pattern.

The Provençal canzon, like the Elizabethan lyric, was written for music. Mr. Pound has more recently insisted, in a series of articles on the work of Arnold Dolmetsch, in the *Egoist*, on the importance of a study of music for the poet.

Such a relation between poetry and music is very different from what is called the 'music' of Shelley or Swinburne, a music often nearer to rhetoric (or the art of the orator) than to the instrument. For poetry to approach the condition of music (Pound quotes approvingly the dictum of Pater) it is not necessary that poetry should be destitute of meaning. Instead of slightly veiled and resonant abstractions, like:

Time with a gift of tears,
Grief with a glass that ran–

of Swinburne, or the mossiness of Mallarmé, Pound's verse is always definite and concrete, because he has always a definite emotion behind it.

Though I've roamed through many places,
None there is that my heart troweth
Fair as that wherein fair groweth
One whose laud here interlaces
Tuneful words, that I've essayed.
Let this tune be gently played
Which my voice herward upraises.

At the end of this poem the author appends the note:

'The form and measure are those of Piere Vidal's "*Ab l'alen tir vas me l'aire.*" The song is fit only to be sung, and is not to be spoken.'

There are, here and there, deliberate archaisms or oddities (e.g., 'herward'); there are deliberately arbitrary images, having their place in the total effect of the poem:

Red leaf that art blown upward and out and over
The green sheaf of the world . . .

The lotos that pours
Her fragrance into the purple cup . . .

Black lightning . . . (in a more recent poem)

but no word is ever chosen merely for the tinkle; each has always its part in producing an impression which is produced always through language. Words are perhaps the hardest of all material of art: for they must be used to express both visual beauty and beauty of sound, as well as communicating a grammatical statement. It would be interesting to compare Pound's use of images with Mallarmé's; I think it will be found that the former's, by the contrast, will appear always sharp in outline, even if arbitrary and not photographic. Such images as those quoted above are as precise in their way as:

Sur le Noel, morte saison,
Lorsque les loups vivent de vent . . .

and the rest of that memorable Testament.

So much for the imagery. As to the 'freedom' of his verse, Pound has made several statements in his articles on Dolmetsch which are to the point:

'Any work of art is a compound of freedom and order. It is perfectly obvious that art hangs between chaos on the one side and mechanics on the other. A pedantic insistence upon detail tends to drive out 'major form'. A firm hold on major form makes for a freedom of detail. In painting men intent on minutiae gradually lost the sense of form and form-combination. An attempt to restore this sense is branded as 'revolution'. It is revolution in the philological sense of the term . . .

'Art is a departure from fixed positions; felicitous departure from a norm . . .'

The freedom of Pound's verse is rather a state of tension due to constant opposition between free and strict. There are not, as a matter of fact, two kinds of verse, the strict and the free; there is only a mastery which comes of being so well trained that form is an instinct and can be adapted to the particular purpose in hand.

After *Exultations* came the translation of the 'Sonnets and Ballate of Guido Cavalcanti'. It is worth noting that the writer of a long review in the *Quest* – speaking in praise of the translation, yet found fault with the author not on the ground of excessive mediaevalism, but because:

'he is concerned rather with the future than with a somewhat remote past, so that in spite of his love for the mediaeval poets, his very accomplishment as a distinctly modern poet makes against his success as a wholly acceptable translator of Cavalcanti, the heir of the Troubadours, the scholastic.

Yet the *Daily News*, in criticizing *Canzoni*, had remarked that Mr. Pound:

'seems to us rather a scholar than a poet, and we should like to see him giving his unusual talent more to direct translation from the Provençal.'

and Mr. J. C. Squire (now the literary editor of the *New Statesman*), in an appreciative review in the *New Age*, had counselled the poet that he would:

'gain and not lose if he could forget all about the poets of Dante's day, their roses and their flames, their gold and their falcons, and their literary amorousness, and walk out of the library into the fresh air.'

In *Ripostes* there are traces of a different idiom. Superfically, the work may appear less important. The diction is more restrained, the flights shorter, the dexterity of technique is less arresting. By romantic readers the book would be considered less 'passionate'. But there is a much more solid substratum to this book; there is more thought; greater depth, if less agitation on the surface. The effect of London is apparent; the author has become a critic of men, surveying them from a consistent and developed point of view; he is more formidable and disconcerting; in short, much more mature. That he abandons nothing of his technical skill is evident from the translation from the Anglo-Saxon, the 'Seafarer'. It is not a slight achievement to have brought to life alliterative verse: perhaps the 'Seafarer' is the only successful piece of alliterative verse ever written in modern English; alliterative verse which is not merely a clever tour de force, but which suggests the possibility of a new development of this form. Mr. Richard Aldington (whose own accomplishments as a writer of vers libre qualify him to speak) called the poem 'unsurpassed and unsurpassable,' and a writer in the *New Age* (a literary organ which has always been strongly opposed to metrical innovations) called it 'one of the finest literary works of art produced in England during the last ten years.' And the rough, stern beauty of the Anglo-Saxon, we may remark, is at the opposite pole from that of the Provençal and Italian poets to whom Pound had previously devoted his attention.

May I for my own self song's truth reckon,
Journey's jargon, how I in harsh days
Hardship endured oft.

But we can notice in *Ripostes* other evidences than of versatility only; certain poems show Mr. Pound turning to more modern subjects, as in the 'Portrait d'une femme,' or the mordant epigram, 'An Object'. Many readers are apt to confuse the maturing of personality with desiccation of the emotions. There is no desiccation in *Ripostes*. This should be evident to anyone who reads carefully such a poem as 'A Girl'. We quote it entire without comment:

The tree has entered my hands,
The sap has ascended my arms,
The tree has grown in my breast—
Downward,
The branches grow out of me, like arms.

Tree you are,
Moss you are,
You are violets with wind above them.
A child–so *high*–*you are,*
And all this is folly to the world.

'The Return' is an important study in verse which is really quantitative. We quote only a few lines:

See, they return; ah, see the tentative
Movements, and the slow feet,
The trouble in the pace and the uncertain
Wavering!

Ripostes belongs to the period when Mr. Pound was being attacked because of his propaganda. He became known as the inventor of 'Imagism', and later, as the 'High Priest of Vorticism'. As a matter of fact, the actual 'propaganda' of Mr. Pound has been very small in quantity. The impression which his personality made, however, is suggested by the following note in *Punch*, which is always a pretty reliable barometer of the English middle-class Grin:

'Mr. Welkin Mark (exactly opposite Long Jane's) begs to announce that he has secured for the English market the palpitating works of the new Montana (U.S.A.) poet, Mr. Ezekiel Ton, who is the most remarkable thing in poetry since Robert Browning. Mr. Ton, who has left America to reside for a while in London and impress his personality on English editors, publishers and readers, is by far the newest poet going, whatever other advertisements may say. He has succeeded, where all others have failed, in evolving a blend of the imagery of the unfettered West, the vocabulary of Wardour Street, and the sinister abandon of Borgiac Italy.'

In 1913, someone writing to the New York *Nation* from the University of Illinois, illustrates the American, more serious, disapproval. This writer begins by expressing his objections to the 'principle of Futurism.' (Pound has perhaps done more than anyone to keep Futurism out of England. His antagonism to this movement was the first which was not due merely to unintelligent dislike for anything new, and was due to his perception that Futurism was incompatible with any principles of form. In his own words, Futurism is 'accelerated impressionism'.) The writer in the *Nation* then goes on to analyse the modern 'hypertrophy of romanticism' into:

'The exaggeration of the importance of a personal emotion
The abandonment of all standards of form
The suppression of all evidence that a particular composition is animated by any directing intelligence.'

As for the first point, here are Mr. Pound's words in answer to the question, 'Do you agree that the great poet is never emotional?'

'Yes, absolutely; if by emotion is meant that he is at the mercy of every passing mood . . . The only kind of emotion worthy of a poet is the inspirational emotion which energizes and strengthens, and which is very remote from the everyday emotion of sloppiness and sentiment . . .'

And as for the platform of Imagism, here are a few of Pound's 'Don'ts for Imagists':

'Pay no attention to the criticisms of men who have never themselves written a notable work.

Use no superfluous word and no adjective which does not reveal something.

Go in fear of abstractions. Don't retail in mediocre verse what has already been done in good prose.

Don't imagine that the art of poetry is any simpler than the art of music or that you can please the expert before you have spent at least as much effort on the art of verse as the average piano teacher spends on the art of music.

'Be influenced by as many great artists as you can, but have the decency either to acknowledge the debt outright or try to conceal it.

'Consider the definiteness of Dante's presentation as compared with Milton's. Read as much of Wordsworth as does not seem to be unutterably dull.

'If you want the gist of the matter go to Sappho, Catullus,

Villon when he is in the vein, Gautier when he is not too frigid, or if you have not the tongues seek out the leisurely Chaucer.

'Good prose will do you no harm. There is good discipline to be had by trying to write it. Translation is also good training.'

The emphasis here is certainly on discipline and form. The Chicago *Tribune* recognized this as 'sound sense', adding:

'If this is Imagism . . . we are for establishing Imagism by constitutional amendment and imprisoning without recourse to ink or paper all "literary" ladies or gents who break any of these canons.'

But other reviewers were less approving. While the writer in the *Nation*, quoted above, dreads the anarchy impending, Mr. William Archer was terrified at the prospect of hieratic formalization. Mr. Archer believes in the simple untaught muse:

'Mr. Pound's commandments tend too much to make of poetry a learned, self-conscious craft, to be cultivated by a guild of adepts, from whose austere laboratories spontaneity and simplicity are excluded . . . A great deal of the best poetry in the world has very little technical study behind it . . . There are scores and hundreds of people in England who could write this simple metre (i.e. of "A Shropshire Lad") successfully.'

To be hanged for a cat and drowned for a rat is, perhaps, sufficient exculpation.

Probably Mr. Pound has won odium not so much by his theories as by his unstinted praise of certain contemporary authors whose work he has liked. Such expressions of approval are usually taken as a grievance—much more so than any personal abuse, which is comparatively a compliment—by the writers who escape his mention. He does not say 'A., B., and C. are bad poets or novelists,' but when he says 'The work of X., Y., and Z. is in such and such respects the most important work in verse (or prose) since so and so,' then A., B., and C. are aggrieved. Also, Pound has frequently expressed disapproval of Milton and Wordsworth.

After *Ripostes* Mr. Pound's idiom has advanced still farther. Inasmuch as *Cathay*, the volume of translations from the Chinese, appeared prior to *Lustra*, it is sometimes thought that his newer idiom is due to the Chinese influence. This is almost the reverse of the truth. The late Ernest Fenollosa left a quantity of manuscripts, including a great number of rough translations (literally exact) from the Chinese. After certain poems subsequently incorporated in *Lustra* had appeared in *Poetry*, Mrs. Fenollosa recognized that in Pound the Chinese manuscripts would find the interpreter whom her husband would have wished: she accordingly forwarded the papers for him to do as he liked with. It is thus due to Mrs. Fenollosa's acumen that we have *Cathay*; it is not as a consequence of *Cathay* that we have *Lustra*. This fact must be borne in mind.

Poems afterwards embodied in *Lustra* appeared in *Poetry*, in April 1913, under the title of *Contemporanea*. They included among others 'Tenzone', 'The Condolence', 'The Garret', 'Salutation the Second', and 'Dance Figure'.

There are influences, but deviously. It is rather a gradual development of experience into which literary experiences have entered. These have not brought the bondage of temporary enthusiasms, but have liberated the poet from his former restricted sphere. There is Catullus and Martial, Gautier, Laforgue and Tristan Corbière. Whitman is certainly not an influence; there is not a trace of him anywhere; Whitman and Mr. Pound are antipodean to each other. Of *Contemporanea* the *Chicago Evening Post* discriminatingly observed:

'Your poems in the April *Poetry* are so mockingly, so delicately, so unblushingly beautiful that you seem to have brought back into the world a grace which (probably) never existed, but which we discover by an imaginative process in Horace and Catullus.'

It was a true insight to ally Pound to the Latin, not to the Greek poets.

Certain of the poems in *Lustra* have offended admirers of the verse of the *Personae* period. When a poet alters or develops, many of his admirers are sure to drop off. Any poet, if he is to survive as a writer beyond his twenty-fifth year, must alter; he must seek new literary influences; he will have different emotions to express. This is disconcerting to that public which likes a poet to spin his whole work out of the feelings of his youth; which likes to be able to open a new volume of his poems with the assurance that they will be able to approach it exactly as they approached the preceding. They do not like that constant readjustment which the following of Mr. Pound's work demands. Thus has *Lustra* been a disappointment to some; though it manifests no falling off in technique, and no impoverishment of feeling. Some of the poems (including several of the *Contemporanea*) are a more direct statement of views than Pound's verse had ever given before. Of these poems, M. Jean de Bosschère writes:

'Everywhere his poems incite man to exist, to profess a becoming egotism, without which there can be no real altruism.

I beseech you enter your life.
I beseech you learn to say "I"
When I question you.
For you are no part, but a whole;
No portion, but a being.

'. . . One must be capable of reacting to stimuli for a moment, as a real, live person, even in face of as much of one's own powers as are arrayed against one; . . . The virile complaint, the revolt of the poet, all which shows his emotion,—that is poetry.

Speak against unconscious oppression,
Speak against the tyranny of the unimaginative,
Speak against bonds.
    Be against all forms of oppression,
    Go out and defy opinion.

'This is the old cry of the poet, but more precise, as an expression of frank disgust:

Go to the adolescent who are smothered in family.
O, how hideous it is
To see three generations of one house gathered together!
It is like an old tree without shoots,
And with some branches rotted and falling.

'Each poem holds out these cries of revolt or disgust, but they are the result of his still hoping and feeling.

'Let us take arms against this sea of stupidities. Pound . . . has experience of the folly of the Philistines who read his verse. Real pain is born of this stupid interpretation, and one does not realize how deep it is unless one can feel, through the ejaculations and the laughter, what has caused these wounds, which are made deeper by what he knows, and what he has lost . . .

'The tone, which is at once jocund and keen, is one of Pound's qualities. Ovid, Catullus–he does not disown them. He only uses these accents for his familiars; with the others he is on the edge of paradox, pamphleteering, indeed of abuse . . .'

This is the proper approach to the poems at the beginning of *Lustra,* and to the short epigrams, which some readers find 'pointless,' or certainly 'not poetry.' They should read, then, the 'Dance Figure', or 'Near Perigord', and remember that all these poems come out of the same man.

Thine arms are as a young sapling under the bark;
Thy face as a river with lights.

White as an almond are thy shoulders;
As new almonds stripped from the husk.

Or the ending of 'Near Perigord':

Bewildering spring, and by the Auvezere
Poppies and day's-eyes in the green email
Rose over us; and we knew all that stream,
And our two horses had traced out the valleys;
Knew the low flooded lands squared out with poplars,
In the young days when the deep sky befriended.
And great wheels in heaven
Bore us together . . . surging . . . and apart . . .
Believing we should meet with lips and hands . . .

There shut up in his castle, Tairiran's,
She who had nor ears nor tongue save in her hands,
Gone, ah, gone—untouched, unreachable!

She who could never live save through one person,
She who could never speak save to one person,
And all the rest of her a shifting change,
A broken bundle of mirrors . . .!

Then turn at once to 'To a Friend Writing on Cabaret Dancers'.

It is easy to say that the language of *Cathay* is due to the Chinese. If one looks carefully at (1) Pound's other verse, (2) other people's translations from the Chinese (e.g. Giles's), it is evident that this is not the case. The language was ready for the Chinese poetry. Compare, for instance, a passage from 'Provincia Deserta':

I have walked
into Perigord
I have seen the torch-flames, high-leaping,
Painting the front of that church,–
And, under the dark, whirling laughter,
I have looked back over the stream
and seen the high building,
Seen the long minarets, the white shafts.
I have gone in Ribeyrac,
and in Sarlat.
I have climbed rickety stairs, heard talk of Croy,
Walked over En Bertrans' old layout,
Have seen Narbonne, and Cahors and Chalus,
Have seen Excideuil, carefully fashioned.

with a passage from 'The River Song':

He goes out to Hori, to look at the wing-flapping storks,
He returns by way of Sei rock, to hear the new nightingales,
For the gardens at Jo-run are full of new nightingales,
Their sound is mixed in this flute,
Their voice is in the twelve pipes here.

It matters very little how much is due to Rihaku and how much to Pound. Mr. Ford Madox Hueffer has observed: 'If these are original verses, then Mr. Pound is the greatest poet of this day.' He goes on to say:

'The poems in *Cathay* are things of a supreme beauty. What poetry should be, that they are. And if a new breath of imagery and handling can do anything for our poetry, that new breath these poems bring . . .

'Poetry consists in so rendering concrete objects that the emotions produced by the objects shall arise in the reader . . .

'Where have you better rendered, or more permanently beautiful a rendering of, the feelings of one of those lonely watchers in the outposts of progress, whether it be Ovid in Hyrcania, a Roman sentinel upon the great wall of this country, or merely ourselves, in the lonely recesses of our minds, than the 'Lament of the Frontier Guard'? . . .

'Beauty is a very valuable thing; perhaps it is the most valuable thing in life; but the power to express emotion so that it shall communicate itself intact and exactly is almost more valuable. Of both these qualities Mr. Pound's book is very full. Therefore, I think we may say that this is much the best work he has done, for, however closely he may have followed his originals–and of that most of us have no means of judging–there is certainly a good deal of Mr. Pound in this little volume.'

Cathay and *Lustra* were followed by the translations of Noh plays. The Noh are not so important as the Chinese poems (certainly not so important for English); the attitude is less unusual to us; the work is not so solid, so firm. *Cathay* will, I believe, rank with the 'Seafarer' in the future among Mr. Pound's original work; the Noh will rank among his translations. It is rather a dessert after *Cathay*. There are, however, passages which, as Pound has handled them, are different both from the Chinese and from anything existent in English. There is, for example, the fine speech of the old Kagekiyo, as he thinks of his youthful valour:

'He thought, how easy this killing. He rushed with his spear-shaft gripped under his arm. He cried out, "I am Kagekiyo of the Heike." He rushed on to take them. He pierced through the helmet vizards of Miyanoya. Miyanoya fled twice, and again; and Kagekiyo cried: "You shall not escape me!" He leaped and wrenched off his helmet. "Eya!" The vizard broke and remained in his hand, and Miyanoya still fled afar, and afar, and he looked back crying in terror, "How terrible, how heavy your arm!" And Kagekiyo called at him, "How tough the shaft of your neck is!" And they both laughed out over the battle, and went off each his own way.'

The Times Literary Supplement spoke of Mr. Pound's 'mastery of beautiful diction' and his 'cunningly rhythmical prose,' in its review of the Noh.

Even since *Lustra* Mr. Pound has moved again. This move is to the epic, of which three cantos appear in the American 'Lustra' (they have already appeared in *Poetry*'–Miss Monroe deserves great honour for her courage in printing an epic poem in this twentieth century–but the version in *Lustra* is revised and is improved by revision). We will leave it as a test: when anyone has studied Mr. Pound's poems in *chronological* order, and has mastered *Lustra* and *Cathay*, he is prepared for the *Cantos*–but not till then. If the reader then fails to like them, he has probably omitted some step in his progress, and had better go back and retrace the journey.

REFLECTIONS ON VERS LIBRE[1]

Ceux qui possèdent leur *vers libre y tiennent: on n'abandonne que* le *vers libre*. DUHAMEL ET VILDRAC.

A lady, renowned in her small circle for the accuracy of her stop-press information of literature, complains to me of a growing pococurantism. 'Since the Russians came in I can read nothing else. I have finished Dostoevski, and I do not know what to do.' I suggested that the great Russian was an admirer of Dickens, and that she also might find that author readable. 'But Dickens is a sentimentalist; Dostoevski is a realist.' I reflected on the amours of Sonia and Rashkolnikov, but forbore to press the point, and I proposed *It Is Never too Late to Mend*. 'But one cannot read the Victorians at all!' While I was extracting the virtues of the proposition that Dostoevski is a Christian, while Charles Reade is merely pious, she added that she could no longer read any verse but *vers libre*.

It is assumed that *vers libre* exists. It is assumed that *vers libre* is a school; that it consists of certain theories; that its group or groups of theorists will either revolutionize or demoralize poetry if their attack upon the iambic pentameter meets with any success. *Vers libre* does not exist, and it is time that this preposterous fiction followed the *élan vital* and the eighty thousand Russians into oblivion.

When a theory of art passes it is usually found that a groat's worth of art has been bought with a million of advertisement. The theory which sold the wares may be quite false, or it may be confused and incapable of elucidation, or it may never have existed. A mythical revolution will have taken place and produced

[1] This article appeared in the *New Statesman*, March 3rd, 1917.

a few works of art which perhaps would be even better if still less of the revolutionary theories clung to them. In modern society such revolutions are almost inevitable. An artist happens upon a method, perhaps quite unreflectingly, which is new in the sense that it is essentially different from that of the second-rate people about him, and different in everything but essentials from that of any of his great predecessors. The novelty meets with neglect; neglect provokes attack; and attack demands a theory. In an ideal state of society one might imagine the good New growing naturally out of the good Old, without the need for polemic and theory; this would be a society with a living tradition. In a sluggish society, as actual societies are, tradition is ever lapsing into superstition, and the violent stimulus of novelty is required. This is bad for the artist and his school, who may become circumscribed by their theory and narrowed by their polemic; but the artist can always console himself for his errors in his old age by considering that if he had not fought nothing would have been accomplished.

Vers libre has not even the excuse of a polemic; it is a battle-cry of freedom, and there is no freedom in art. And as the so-called *vers libre* which is good is anything but 'free', it can better be defended under some other label. Particular types of *vers libre* may be supported on the choice of content, or on the method of handling the content. I am aware that many writers of *vers libre* have introduced such innovations, and that the novelty of their choice and manipulation of material is confused—if not in their own minds, in the minds of many of their readers—with the novelty of the form. But I am not here concerned with imagism, which is a theory about the use of material; I am only concerned with the theory of the verse-form in which imagism is cast. If *vers libre* is a genuine verse-form it will have a positive definition. And I can define it only in negatives: (1) absence of pattern, (2) absence of rhyme, (3) absence of metre.

The third of these qualities is easily disposed of. What sort of a line that would be which would not scan at all I cannot say. Even in the popular American magazines, whose verse columns are now largely given over to *vers libre*, the lines are usually explicable in terms of prosody. Any line can be divided into feet and accents. The simpler metres are a repetition of one combination, perhaps a long and a short, or a short and a long syllable, five times repeated. There is, however, no reason why, within the single line, there should be any repetition; why there should not be lines (as there are) divisible only into feet of different types. How can the grammatical exercise of scansion make a line of this sort more intelligible? Only by isolating elements which occur in other lines, and the sole purpose of doing this is the production of a similar effect elsewhere. But repetition of effect is a question of pattern.

Scansion tells us very little. It is probable that there is not much to be gained by an elaborate system of prosody, by the erudite complexities of Swinburnian metre. With Swinburne, once the trick is perceived and the scholarship appreciated, the effect is somewhat diminished. When the unexpectedness, due to the unfamiliarity of the metres to English ears, wears off and is understood, one ceases to look for what one does not find in Swinburne; the inexplicable line with the music which can never be recaptured in other words. Swinburne mastered his technique, which is a great deal, but he did not master it to the extent of being able to take liberties with it, which is everything. If anything promising for English poetry is hidden in the metres of Swinburne, it probably lies far beyond the point to which Swinburne has developed them. But the most interesting verse which has yet been written in our language has been done either by taking a very simple form, like the iambic pentameter, and constantly withdrawing from it, or taking no form at all, and constantly approximating to a very simple one. It is this contrast between fixity and flux, this unperceived evasion of monotony, which is the very life of verse.

I have in mind two passages of contemporary verse which would be called *vers libre*. Both of them I quote because of their beauty:

> *Once, in finesse of fiddles found I ecstasy,*
> *In the flash of gold heels on the hard pavement.*
> *Now see I*

That warmth's the very stuff of poesy.
Oh, God, make small
The old star-eaten blanket of the sky,
That I may fold it round me and in comfort lie.

This is a complete poem. The other is part of a much longer poem:

There shut up in his castle, Tairiran's,
She who had nor ears nor tongue save in her hands,
Gone—ah, gone—untouched, unreachable!
She who could never live save through one person,
She who could never speak save to one person,
And all the rest of her a shifting change,
A broken bundle of mirrors . . . !

It is obvious that the charm of these lines could not be, without the constant suggestion and the skilful evasion of iambic pentameter.

At the beginning of the seventeenth century, and especially in the verse of John Webster, who was in some ways a more cunning technician than Shakespeare, one finds the same constant evasion and recognition of regularity. Webster is much freer than Shakespeare, and that his fault is not negligence is evidenced by the fact that his verse acquires this freedom. That there is also carelessness I do not deny, but the irregularity of carelessness can be at once detected from the irregularity of deliberation. (In *The White Devil* Brachiano dying, and Cornelia mad, deliberately rupture the bonds of pentameter.)

I recover, like a spent taper, for a flash
and instantly go out.

Cover her face; mine eyes dazzle; she died young.

You have cause to love me, I did enter you in my heart
Before you would vouchsafe to call for the keys.

This is a vain poetry: but I pray you tell me
If there were proposed me, wisdom, riches, and beauty,
In three several young men, which should I choose?

These are not lines of carelessness. The irregularity is further enhanced by the use of short lines and the breaking up of lines in dialogue, which alters the quantities. And there are many lines in the drama of this time which are spoilt by regular accentuation.

> *I loved this woman in spite of my heart.* (The Changeling)
> *I would have these herbs grow up in his grave.* (The White Devil)
> *Whether the spirit of greatness or of woman . . .* (The Duchess of Malfi)

The general charge of decadence cannot be preferred. Tourneur and Shirley, who I think will be conceded to have touched nearly the bottom of the decline of tragedy, are much more regular than Webster or Middleton. Tourneur will polish off a fair line of iambics even at the cost of amputating a preposition from its substantive, and in the *Atheist's Tragedy* he has a final 'of' in two lines out of five together.

We may therefore formulate as follows: the ghost of some simple metre should lurk behind the arras in even the 'freest' verse; to advance menacingly as we doze, and withdraw as we rouse. Or, freedom is only truly freedom when it appears against the background of an artificial limitation.

Not to have perceived the simple truth that *some* artificial limitation is necessary except in moments of the first intensity is, I believe, a capital error of even so distinguished a talent as that of Mr. E. L. Masters. The *Spoon River Anthology* is not material of the first intensity; it is reflective, not immediate; its author is a moralist, rather than an observer. His material is so near to the material of Crabbe that one wonders why he should have used a different form. Crabbe is, on the whole, the more intense of the two; he is keen, direct, and unsparing. His material is prosaic, not in the sense that it would have been better done in prose, but in the sense of requiring a simple and rather rigid verse-form, and this Crabbe has given it. Mr. Masters requires a more rigid verse-form than either of the two contemporary poets quoted above, and his epitaphs suffer from the lack of it.

So much for metre. There is no escape from metre; there is only mastery. But while there obviously is escape from rhyme, the *vers librists* are by no means the first out of the cave.

The boughs of the trees
Are twisted
By many bafflings;
Twisted are
The small-leafed boughs.
But the shadow of them
Is not the shadow of the mast head
Nor of the torn sails.

When the white dawn first
Through the rough fir-planks
Of my hut, by the chestnuts,
Up at the valley-head,
Came breaking, Goddess,
I sprang up, I threw round me
My dappled fawn-skin . . .

Except for the more human touch in the second of these extracts a hasty observer would hardly realize that the first is by a contemporary, and the second by Matthew Arnold.

I do not minimize the services of modern poets in exploiting the possibilities of rhymeless verse. They prove the strength of a Movement, the utility of a Theory. What neither Blake nor Arnold could do alone is being done in our time. 'Blank verse' is the only accepted rhymeless verse in English–the inevitable iambic pentameter. The English ear is (or was) more sensitive to the music of the verse and less dependent upon the recurrence of identical sounds in this metre than in any other. There is no campaign against rhyme. But it is possible that excessive devotion to rhyme has thickened the modern ear. The rejection of rhyme is not a leap at facility; on the contrary, it imposes a much severer strain upon the language. When the comforting echo of rhyme is removed, success or failure in the choice of words, in the sentence structure, in the order, is at once more apparent. Rhyme removed, the poet is at once held up to the standards of prose. Rhyme removed, much ethereal music leaps up from the word, music which has hitherto chirped unnoticed in the expanse of prose. Any rhyme forbidden, many Shagpats were unwigged.

And this liberation from rhyme might be as well a liberation *of* rhyme. Freed from its exacting task of supporting lame verse, it could be applied with greater effect where it is most needed. There are often passages in an unrhymed poem where rhyme is wanted for some special effect, for a sudden tightening-up, for a cumulative insistence, or for an abrupt change of mood. But formal rhymed verse will certainly not lose its place. We only need the coming of a Satirist—no man of genius is rarer—to prove that the heroic couplet has lost none of its edge since Dryden and Pope laid it down. As for the sonnet I am not so sure. But the decay of intricate formal patterns has nothing to do with the advent of *vers libre*. It had set in long before. Only in a closely-knit and homogeneous society, where many men are at work on the same problems, such a society as those which produced the Greek chorus, the Elizabethan lyric, and the Troubadour canzone, will the development of such forms ever be carried to perfection. And as for *vers libre*, we conclude that it is not defined by absence of pattern or absence of rhyme, for other verse is without these; that it is not defined by non-existence of metre, since even the *worst* verse can be scanned; and we conclude that the division between Conservative Verse and *vers libre* does not exist, for there is only good verse, bad verse, and chaos.